MARQUEE
SERIES

MICROSOFT®
Windows® 98

MEREDITH FLYNN
Bowling Green State University
Bowling Green, Ohio

ANN MILLER
Columbus State Community College
Columbus, Ohio

 EMCParadigm

CONTENTS

The Marquee Series Team: Sonja Brown, Senior Editor; Joan D'Onofrio, Art Director; Jennifer Wreisner, Cover Designer; Leslie Anderson, Text Designer and Desktop Production Specialist; Desiree Faulkner and Susan Capecchi, Testers; Sharon O'Donnell and Courtney Kost, Proofreaders; Nancy Fulton, Indexer.

The Publishing Team: George Provol, Publisher; Janice Johnson, Director of Product Development; Lori Landwer, Marketing Manager; Shelley Clubb, Electronic Design and Production Manager.

Registered Trademarks: Microsoft and Windows are registered trademarks of Microsoft Corporation in the United States and other countries.

Acknowledgment: The authors and publisher wish to thank Patricia Partyka, Schoolcraft College, Livonia, MI, for technical and academic assistance.

Library of Congress Cataloging-in-Publication Data
Flynn, Meredith.
  Microsoft Windows 98 / Meredith Flynn, Ann Miller.
      p. cm.—(Marquee Series)
  ISBN 0-7638-0401-0 (text)
  1. Microsoft Windows (Computer file) 2. Operating systems (Computer file) I. Miller,
Ann, 1949- II. Title. III. Series

  QA76.76.063 F5982 2000
  005.4'469—dc21   00-032105

© 2001 by Paradigm Publishing Inc.
Published by **EMC**Paradigm   (800) 535-6865
          875 Montreal Way   E-mail: educate@emcp.com
          St. Paul, MN 55102   Web Site: www.emcp.com

Printed in the United States of America   10 9 8 7 6 5 4 3 2 1

Introducing the Windows 98 Operating System

An operating system is a program that gives the computer a set of instructions on how to load software, initialize devices, manage memory, and do the other "behind-the-scenes" operations necessary for the computer to run. *Software* is a program that you use to perform a specific function. Microsoft Word, for example, is a software program used to perform word processing functions. When the operating system *initializes* devices, it prepares the devices to receive instructions from the operating system. The initialization process includes checking to see that all devices are connected properly. *Memory*, also known as RAM (Random Access Memory), is where the computer stores information as it is being processed. This type of memory is temporary, and its contents are erased when the computer is shut down. *Storage*, such as a hard disk or floppy disk, stores information permanently. Information is stored when you save it using the software's Save command.

Windows 98 is an operating system with a graphical user interface (GUI—pronounced "gooey") that offers integration with the Internet and support for a large number of peripheral devices. Learning the basic features and functions of Windows 98 will give you a better understanding of how your application software works and therefore will allow you to master applications such as the Office 2000 suite much more quickly. In this section, you will learn the following skills:

Skills

- Start and shut down Windows 98
- Identify desktop components
- Use the mouse
- Open and close windows
- Move windows
- Resize windows

- Minimize, maximize, and restore windows
- Switch between open windows
- Select options from menus and toolbars
- Select options in dialog boxes

Starting and Shutting Down Windows; Identifying Desktop Components

Windows 98 starts automatically when your computer is turned on. Depending on your system configuration, you may need to enter a network password or a Windows password. When you are finished working in Windows and want to turn your computer off, you should go through the Windows shutdown procedure. The Windows operating system uses many system files and resources while it is running. If these files and resources are not closed properly, data can be corrupted or you may encounter system start-up problems. With both starting and shutting down Windows, you will use a *mouse*, a device connected to the computer and placed on a flat surface, usually a *mouse pad*. A mouse typically has two buttons, although some have three. Tapping the buttons executes specific functions and commands. Five functions are performed with the mouse: *click, double-click, drag, right-click*, and *scroll*. Depending on the location of the pointer on the screen, your mouse pointer will appear in various shapes.

steps

(Note: Several display options are available for the Windows 98 desktop. Exercises in the two Windows sections in this book assume you are using the default display, which is <u>Web</u> style. If you need to change the desktop display, refer to the Take 2 at the end of this topic. Exercises in this book also assume you are using a two-button mouse.)

1 Turn on your computer. If it is already running, you should see a screen similar to the one shown in Figure WIN1.1, which represents the Windows desktop area. (Your desktop may look different.)

The desktop area is the main portion of the screen that displays when Windows is loaded. It is similar to a traditional office desktop in that the objects you work with frequently are placed on the desktop.

FIGURE WIN1.1 Windows 98 Desktop

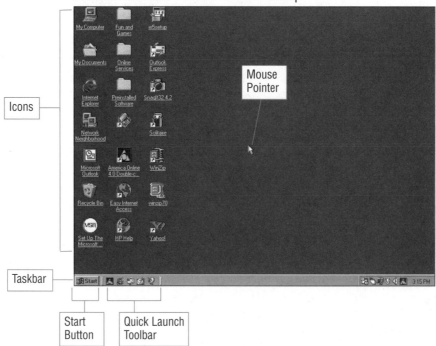

Icons

Mouse Pointer

Taskbar

Start Button

Quick Launch Toolbar

(2) Move the mouse (represented by a white mouse pointer on the screen) around the desktop area.

Figure WIN1.2 illustrates the two mouse configurations and the proper way to hold a mouse. The mouse pointer changes appearance depending on the function being performed or where the pointer is positioned. Table WIN1.1 shows the different images and the locations or situations in which they appear.

FIGURE WIN1.2 Mouse Styles and How to Hold the Mouse

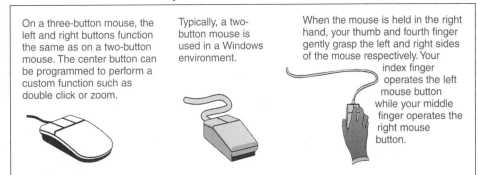

On a three-button mouse, the left and right buttons function the same as on a two-button mouse. The center button can be programmed to perform a custom function such as double click or zoom.

Typically, a two-button mouse is used in a Windows environment.

When the mouse is held in the right hand, your thumb and fourth finger gently grasp the left and right sides of the mouse respectively. Your index finger operates the left mouse button while your middle finger operates the right mouse button.

TABLE WIN1.1 Mouse Pointer Images

Pointer Image	Location
I	Within a text box or an editing window
↖	Pointing to an icon or another item
✛	Positioned over a graphic image or another moveable object
↔	Positioned at a corner or side of a sizable image

(3) Right-click (click the right mouse button once) on an empty area of the desktop to display a shortcut menu.

Right-clicking the mouse in any Windows application will display context-sensitive shortcut menus.

(4) Press the Esc key in the upper left corner of your keyboard to remove the shortcut menu.

Step 3

Active Desktop ▶
Arrange Icons ▶
Line Up Icons
Refresh
Paste
Paste Shortcut
Undo Copy
New ▶
Properties

(continued)

(5) Position the mouse pointer over the time at the right edge of the Taskbar.

The current date will appear above the time in a yellow box. This is referred to as a *Tooltip*. Tooltips provide information about the object or button on which the pointer is currently resting.

Step 5

Problem

If you run out of room on your mouse pad, simply pick up the mouse and reposition it.

(6) Position the mouse pointer on the Quick Launch toolbar.

Programs located on the Quick Launch toolbar can be opened quickly by clicking the icon.

(7) Position the mouse pointer on the Start button.

A Tooltip appears that says *Click here to begin*. The Start button is the starting point for performing tasks in Windows 98.

Step 7

(8) With the mouse pointer resting on the Start button, click the left mouse button.

This action displays the Start menu.

(9) Click a blank area of the desktop to remove the Start menu.

(10) Locate the icon on the desktop called *Recycle Bin*. Position the mouse pointer on the icon and then click the left mouse button.

Step 10

This opens the Recycle Bin window, which lists the files you have deleted from your computer and offers various options for handling the files.

(11) With the Recycle Bin window open, position your mouse pointer on the window's blue title bar, press and hold down the left mouse button, drag the window to a new location on the desktop, and then release the mouse button.

Drag means to press and hold down the left mouse button while moving an item to another location on the screen and then releasing the button at the new location.

Step 11

Problem

If the Recycle Bin window currently fills up the entire screen, then the window has been maximized. Click the Restore button ▣ to complete step 11.

⑫ Close the Recycle Bin window by positioning the mouse pointer on the Close button ⊠ that displays in the upper right corner of the window and then clicking the left mouse button.

Step 12

In the next step you will learn how to shut down Windows.

⑬ Click the Start button.

⑭ At the Start menu, click Shut Down.

⑮ Review the options in the Shut Down Windows dialog box.

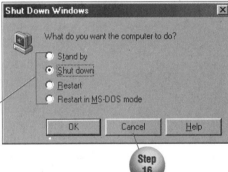

Clicking Shut down will start the shut down process, and, depending on your computer system, may power off the system. Other options at the Shut Down Windows dialog box include Restart (also called a *warm boot*), which restarts your system, and Restart in MS-DOS Mode, which bypasses Windows and takes you directly to a DOS (Disk Operating System) prompt. The Stand by option will turn off the monitor and hard disks. This means the computer uses less power. When the computer comes out of standby, the desktop is restored exactly as it was left. The Stand by option is useful for conserving battery power in laptop computers.

Step 13

Step 14

⑯ Click the Cancel button in the Shut Down Windows dialog box.

Step 15

Step 16

Changing Windows 98 Display Options

Take **2**

During a typical installation of Windows 98, certain defaults or standards are applied to the program. In some situations, Windows 98 may be customized by the manufacturer of the computer hardware or by the computer user. Windows 98 displays in the Web style by default. Exercises in this topic and other Windows topics assume this default. You can check to determine your current display by completing these steps: Click the *My Computer* icon on the Windows 98 desktop. At the My Computer window, click View on the Menu bar and then click Folder Options. At the Folder Options dialog box with the General tab selected shown at the right, look at the currently selected option in the Windows Desktop Update section. To change your display to Web style, click the Web Style option, and then click OK. Close the My Computer window by clicking the Close button (displays with an X) that displays in the upper right corner of the window.

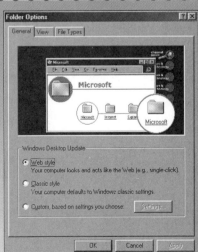

Working with Application Windows

Programs that run under Windows 98 open in an *application window*. An application window is a rectangular area that sits on top of the desktop. A window can display an application (program), documents, or the contents of a disk drive or network drive. Application windows can be moved, resized, maximized, and minimized. Application windows have many features in common, such as menu bars and toolbars. Regardless of what type of window you open, it has a Title bar. A Title bar is the horizontal bar at the top of the window, usually displayed in blue. Look at this bar to determine the name of the application running in the current window or the name of the open file. Programs can be started, or launched, in two ways: from the Start menu (click on the program name in the Programs side menu) and from the desktop (click the program icon, if available). Starting a program is perhaps the most common task performed with Windows 98.

steps

1 At the Windows 98 desktop, click the *My Computer* icon to display the My Computer window.

2 Increase the size of the My Computer window by positioning the mouse pointer at the right edge of the window until it turns into a double-headed arrow pointing left and right. Hold down the left mouse button, drag to the right approximately one inch, and then release the mouse button.

Drag any border of a window to resize it. If you point at a window corner, the mouse pointer changes to a diagonal double-headed arrow, indicating the window will be resized both horizontally and vertically as you drag the mouse.

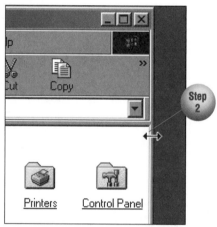

3 Position the mouse pointer on the bottom edge of the window until it turns into a double-headed arrow pointing up and down. Hold down the left mouse button, drag down approximately one inch, and then release the mouse button.

4 Click the Maximize button located at the right side of the Title bar to maximize the My Computer window.

The window fills the entire screen.

5 Click the Restore button located at the right side of the Title bar to return the window to its previous size.

When a window is maximized, the Maximize button changes to the Restore button.

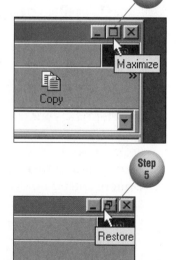

6 Click the Minimize button ▬ to reduce the window to a button on the Taskbar.

7 Click the *Recycle Bin* icon to open the Recycle Bin window.

8 Click the Minimize button to reduce the window to a button on the Taskbar.

Step 6

The Taskbar should now contain two buttons: My Computer and Recycle Bin.

9 Click the button on the Taskbar representing the My Computer window.

The My Computer window is restored to the desktop.

10 Click the button on the Taskbar representing the Recycle Bin.

The Recycle Bin window is restored to the desktop and overlaps the My Computer window. More than one window can be open at the same time. However, only one window will be *active*. The active window is the window with the blue title bar. To activate another window, simply click inside the other window.

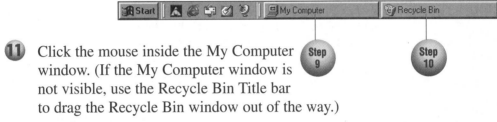

11 Click the mouse inside the My Computer window. (If the My Computer window is not visible, use the Recycle Bin Title bar to drag the Recycle Bin window out of the way.)

Step 9

Step 10

The My Computer window moves to the foreground and the Recycle Bin window moves to the background.

12 Click the Close button ✕ located at the right side of the Title bar to close the My Computer window.

13 Click the Close button at the right side of the Recycle Bin Title bar to close the Recycle Bin window.

Take 2

Switching Between Windows
In this topic you have learned to switch between open windows by clicking the button on the Taskbar for the window that you want to switch to, or by clicking the mouse in an open window in the background of the desktop. As more windows are opened, the buttons on the Taskbar representing each window become smaller and it may become difficult to tell which button represents the window that you want to move to. In this case, you can cycle through a list of open windows by holding down the Alt key and pressing Tab. Continue to hold down the Alt key and press and release Tab to view the next open window name displayed in the middle of the desktop. Release the Alt key when you see the name of the open window that you want to activate.

Using Menus and Toolbars

The functions and capabilities of Windows 98 and applications running under Windows 98 are accessed primarily through menus or toolbars. Typically, a menu bar appears directly under the window's title bar. Each menu item displays as a single word, with one underlined letter. Menus are organized into groups of related commands that are similar among applications. Toolbars typically display below the menu. Depending on the application, there may be multiple toolbars displayed and they may be displayed horizontally or vertically. Toolbars include buttons that represent commands and functions. You can usually customize toolbars by adding or removing buttons from the bar. When you position your mouse pointer over any of the buttons on the toolbar, a ToolTip displays briefly, describing the button's function.

steps

1 Click the *My Computer* icon to open the My Computer window.

2 Click File on the Menu bar and a drop-down menu displays.

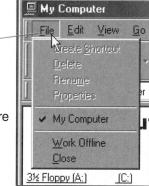

Notice that some of the options on the drop-down menu are dimmed, or gray in color, which means those options are not currently available.

3 Click a blank area of the window to remove the File drop-down menu.

4 Hold down the Alt key on the keyboard, press once on the letter V on the keyboard, and then release the Alt key. This displays the View drop-down menu.

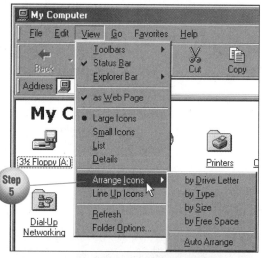

The underlined letter of the option on the Menu bar identifies what letter to press on the keyboard while holding down the Alt key to display the drop-down menu. Notice that some options on the View drop-down menu display with a right-pointing triangle next to the option. This triangle indicates that a side menu is available.

5 Position the mouse pointer on the Arrange Icons option and a side menu displays.

6 Click in a blank area of the window to remove the menu and side menu.

7 Click Edit on the Menu bar.

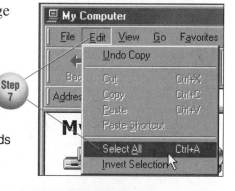

Notice the Select All command has shortcut keystrokes listed beside it. Shortcut commands provide an alternative method for executing commands or features.

(8) Click in a blank area of the window to remove the Edit drop-down menu.

(9) Press Ctrl + A, the Select All shortcut command, to select all the items in the My Computer window.

(10) Click in a blank area of the window to deselect the items.

(11) Click View in the Menu bar.

Notice that Folder Options at the bottom of the menu has an ellipsis (...) next to it. An ellipsis indicates that clicking the option will display a dialog box offering options for how the command is carried out.

(12) Click Folder Options and the Folder Options dialog box displays.

Notice the choices offered by this dialog box.

(13) Click the Cancel button to remove the Folder Options dialog box and return to the My Computer window. Make sure the Properties button is visible on the My Computer toolbar. If it is not, increase the width of the window until the Properties button displays.

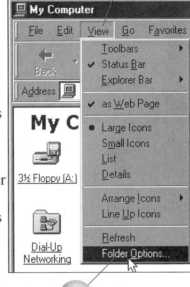

(14) Point to the (C:) icon in the My Computer window.

Pointing to an icon selects it. The (C:) icon usually represents your hard disk drive.

(15) Click once on the Properties button on the toolbar to display the Properties dialog box.

You should see a display of the total amount of storage space (typically in gigabytes, or GB) available on your hard drive compared with the amount of space used to date.

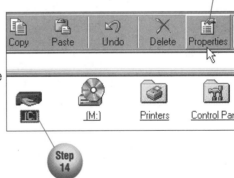

(16) Click the Cancel button to remove the Properties dialog box.

(17) Click the Close button to close the My Computer window.

Displaying Additional Toolbars

If you are working in an application and no toolbars display, click View on the Menu bar and then look for the option *Toolbars*. Point to *Toolbars* and toolbars that are available with the application display in a drop-down list. Click the desired toolbar.

Exploring Dialog Boxes

Windows 98 often needs additional information from the user before it can complete a task. It gets this information through dialog boxes. The appearance and content of dialog boxes varies, depending on the application currently running. However, several elements are common to most dialog boxes, including tabs, text boxes, drop-down lists, option buttons, check boxes, sliders, spinners, and command buttons.

steps

1. Click the *My Computer* icon on the desktop and then click the *Control Panel* icon at the My Computer window.

2. At the Control Panel window, click the *Display* icon.

   This displays the Display Properties dialog box with the Background tab selected. Refer to Figure WIN1.3 for a display of the various dialog box components and then refer to Table WIN1.2 for a description of the components.

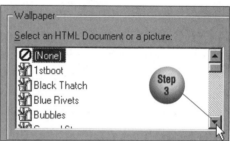

3. View the various wallpapers available by clicking the down-pointing triangle at the bottom of the vertical scroll bar at the right side of the Select an HTML Document or a picture list box.

   When all choices in a list box are not visible, a vertical scroll bar is inserted at the right side of the list box. Use this vertical scroll bar to scroll through the list.

4. Click the Screen Saver tab located towards the top of the dialog box.

   Refer to Table WIN1.2 for a description of tabs.

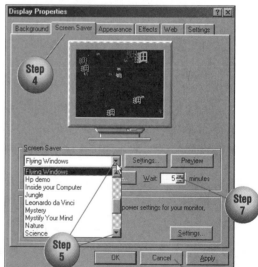

5. Display a drop-down list of screen savers by clicking the down-pointing triangle at the right side of the Screen Saver box. Scroll down the list by clicking the down-pointing triangle.

6. Click anywhere in the dialog box (outside the drop-down list) to remove the drop-down list.

7. Notice the spinners located at the right side of the Wait text box. Click the up-pointing triangle to increase the number and then click the down-pointing triangle to decrease the number. Return to the number that appeared in the text box when you first displayed the dialog box.

   Refer to Table WIN1.2 for a description of spinners. Notice the command buttons—OK, Cancel, and Apply—that display along the bottom of the dialog box.

(8) Click the Cancel button to remove the Display Properties dialog box.

(9) At the My Computer window, click the *Mouse* icon.

You may need to scroll down the list to display the *Mouse* icon.

(10) Notice the two option buttons that display toward the top of the Mouse Properties dialog box. Only one option can be selected at one time. (More than likely, <u>R</u>ight-handed option is selected. Click the <u>L</u>eft-handed option if you use the mouse with your left hand.)

(11) Drag the slider on the slider bar located in the <u>D</u>ouble-click speed section to adjust the speed of double-clicking.

(12) Click the Cancel button to remove the Mouse Properties dialog box.

(13) Click the Close button to close the Control Panel window.

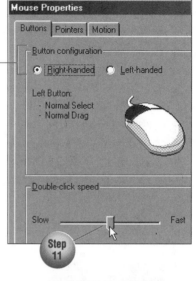

FIGURE WIN1.3 Dialog Box Components

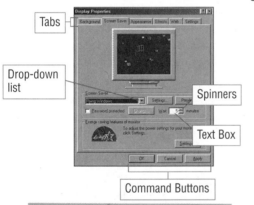

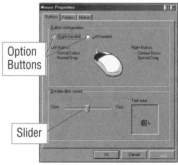

TABLE WIN1.2 Dialog Box Components

Component	Description
Tabs	Think of tabs as "pages." Each tab, or page, presents a group of related options from which you can choose. The active tab is the one in front, and the tab name is surrounded with a thin, gray border. To move to another tab, click the tab name.
Text Boxes	Also called *edit boxes*, these boxes are locations where you key information. If data already displays in the text box, drag to select it, and then key the information.
List Boxes	List boxes present several options in a list format. Click the desired option.
Drop-Down Lists	This special type of list box looks similar to a list box but has a down-pointing triangle at the right side. Click this triangle to display the items in the list.
Option Buttons	Sometimes called *radio buttons*, option buttons present a set of mutually exclusive choices, meaning that only one option (button) in a group of buttons can be selected at one time.
Check Boxes	Check boxes are independent of one another, meaning that more than one can be selected at one time.
Sliders	Use sliders to adjust settings by dragging on a sliding bar until you get the result you want.
Spinners	A spinner is a set of arrows, one pointing up and the other pointing down that allow you to increment or decrement the value of an option.
Command Buttons	Command buttons execute the command listed on the button, usually with no further input from you.

Features Summary

Action	Button	Steps
Display Start menu	Start	
Display Recycle Bin		Click *Recycle Bin* icon on desktop
Shutdown Windows		Click Start, Sh<u>u</u>t Down, <u>S</u>hut down
Display My Computer window		Click *My Computer* icon on desktop
Minimize window	—	
Maximize window	□	
Close window	X	Click <u>F</u>ile, <u>C</u>lose
Select all		Click <u>E</u>dit, Select A<u>l</u>l or press Ctrl + A
Display Folder Options dialog box		In My Computer window, click <u>V</u>iew, Folder <u>O</u>ptions
Display Control Panel window		In My Computer window, click Control Panel icon

Procedures Check

Answer the following questions in the space provided.

1. How does the mouse pointer appear when it is pointing to an icon or other item?

   as an arrow

2. How does the mouse pointer appear when it is positioned at the corner or side of a sizable image?

   as a double arrow

3. What icon would you click on the desktop to display a list of files you have deleted from your hard drive?

   recycle bin

4. What button would you click to reduce the current window to a button on the Taskbar?

   minimize button □

5. What button would you click to expand the current window to fill the entire screen?

   full screen button

6. When you see an ellipsis (...) after a menu item, what does it mean?

   means there is more

7. What does a right-pointing triangle next to a menu item indicate?

   another drop menu

8. What do you call buttons in a dialog box that present a set of mutually exclusive choices?

   tool bar

9. What do you call the up- and down-pointing triangles you can use in a dialog box to increment or decrement the value of an option?

   draging arrow

Skills Review

Note: In some of the following activities you will be instructed to open Network Neighborhood. If you do not have this icon on your desktop, substitute Internet Explorer wherever you see Network Neighborhood.

Activity 1: Opening; Minimizing; Switching Between Windows; Closing Windows

1 Open the My Computer window and then minimize it.
2 Open the Recycle Bin window and then minimize it.
3 Open the Network Neighborhood window.
4 Click the button on the Taskbar representing My Computer.
5 Click the Network Neighborhood window that is behind My Computer.
6 Minimize the Network Neighborhood window.
7 Click the button on the Taskbar representing the Recycle Bin.
8 Click the My Computer window that is behind the Recycle Bin.
9 Close the My Computer window.
10 Close the Recycle Bin window.
11 Right-click the button on the Taskbar representing Network Neighborhood and then click <u>C</u>lose at the shortcut menu.

Activity 2: Moving and Resizing Windows

1 Open the My Computer window.
2 Resize the My Computer window until it is approximately 1/3 the size of your desktop.
3 Move the My Computer window to the upper right corner of the desktop.
4 Open the Recycle Bin window.
5 Resize the Recycle Bin window until it is approximately one-third the size of your desktop.
6 Move the Recycle Bin window to the top left corner of the desktop.
7 Open the Network Neighborhood window. (*If necessary, minimize a window to see the icons behind it.*)
8 Resize the Network Neighborhood window until it is approximately one-third the size of your desktop.
9 Move the Network Neighborhood window to the bottom center of the desktop.
10 Close the Network Neighborhood, My Computer, and Recycle Bin windows.

Activity 3: Using Menus and Dialog Boxes

1 Open the My Computer window.
2 Click <u>V</u>iew on the Menu bar and then click <u>D</u>etails.
3 Click <u>V</u>iew on the Menu bar and then click Large Icons.
4 Click the *Control Panel* icon to open the Control Panel window.
5 Click the *Keyboard* icon in the Control Panel window.
6 With the Speed tab selected in the Keyboard Properties dialog box, drag the <u>R</u>epeat rate slider bar to the left toward Slow.

7 Click in the Click here and hold down a key to test repeat rate text box and hold down an alphabetic key on the keyboard. Notice the rate at which the key repeats.

8 Drag the Repeat rate slider bar to the right towards Fast.

9 Click in the Click here and hold down a key to test repeat rate text box and hold down an alphabetic key on the keyboard. Notice the increase in speed with which the key repeats.

10 Position the Repeat rate slider bar at a speed with which you will be comfortable when holding down a key on the keyboard.

11 Click OK.

12 Click the *Date/Time* icon.

13 With the Date & Time tab selected in the Date/Time Properties dialog box, click the down-pointing triangle to the right of the current month and then click your birthday month in the drop-down list.

14 Use the spinners (triangles) to change the year to 2025.

15 Check which day of the week your birthday falls on in the year 2025.

16 Click the Cancel button in the Date/Time Properties dialog box.

17 Close the Control Panel window.

Performance Plus

Activity 1: Opening and Switching Between Windows; Closing Windows

1 Click the Start button on the Taskbar, point to Programs, and then click Windows Explorer.

2 Click the Start button on the Taskbar, point to Programs, point to Accessories, and then click Address Book.

3 Click the Start button on the Taskbar, point to Programs, point to Accessories, and then click Calculator.

4 Activate Windows Explorer and then close it.

5 Activate Address Book and then close it.

6 Close Calculator.

Activity 2: Moving and Resizing Windows

1 Look at the screen shown in Figure WIN1.4.

2 Arrange your desktop to resemble Figure WIN1.4 as closely as possible.

3 Print a screen capture of your desktop by completing the following steps:

a Press the Print Screen key on the keyboard. This key is usually located at the top right of the keyboard next to the last function key.

b Click Start, point to Programs, point to Accessories, and then click Paint.

c Click Edit and then click Paste. Click Yes if prompted to enlarge the bitmap.

d Click File and then click Print.

e Click OK in the Print dialog box.

f Click File and then click Exit. Click No when prompted to save changes.

4 Close all of the windows.

FIGURE WIN1.4 Activity 2

Introducing the Windows 98 Operating System

Windows® 98
Managing Files and Customizing Windows

File management on a computer is similar to file management in a typical office. By learning how Windows manages files, you are on your way to understanding the basic operations and functions of computers. Using Windows Explorer, you can create your own personal "filing system" on your computer and have complete control over how your documents are stored. You can also move files from one folder to another, copy files from the hard drive to a floppy disk (or do the reverse), and delete and rename files and folders. Windows "out of the box" is a comprehensive program offering logical options for organizing and manipulating information. However, each of us has our own way of working and our own preferences. Recognizing that, Microsoft has designed Windows to allow you to customize the way it displays its functions and features. In this section, you will learn the following skills:

Skills

- Change the View options in Windows Explorer
- Create, rename, and delete a folder
- Collapse and expand folder lists
- Copy and paste a file
- Delete and restore files using the Recycle Bin
- Find files
- Open and run multiple programs at one time
- Browse disks and devices using My Computer
- Customize the appearance of the Desktop and the Start menu
- Create a shortcut
- Set the date and time
- Create an image in Paint
- Create a document in WordPad
- Use the Help feature

Using Windows Explorer

Computers store files in a manner similar to a traditional paper-based filing system. A traditional filing system has file cabinets, drawers, files, and folders. Windows has multiple drives, folders on those drives, and files within the folders. In each system, a document (or file) is the smallest unit of data. Using Windows' file management tools, you can control and organize your data files in a way that is meaningful to you. Operating system and program files, however, should not be moved or removed by a typical user. With Windows Explorer, you can create folders, move folders, and rename folders. You also can move, copy, rename, and delete files. When you open Explorer, your files are displayed in the right pane with these column headings: Name, Size, Type, and Modified. Folders are always displayed first, in alphabetical order, and files are displayed in alphabetical order after the folders. By clicking on a column heading, you can sort the column in the opposite order.

steps

(Note: Before completing the steps in this topic and the remaining topics in this section, the Windows Data Files folder and its contents must be available on your computer's hard drive. This folder can be downloaded from the EMC/Paradigm Web site, or you may get it from your instructor.)

1 Click the Start button on the Taskbar and then point to Programs.

When you point to Programs, a side menu displays.

2 At the side menu, click *Windows Explorer*.

Figure WIN2.1 shows the Windows Explorer window. See Table WIN2.1 for a list of the components and their functions.

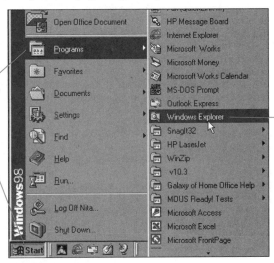

Step 1

Step 2

Problem

? If your Windows Explorer window does not display toolbars, click <u>V</u>iew and then <u>T</u>oolbars on the Menu bar. Click the toolbar you wish to display (you will see a check mark next to the toolbar name).

FIGURE WIN2.1 Windows Explorer

Title Bar

Menu Bar

Standard Toolbar

Address Bar

Folders Pane

Status Bar

Links Toolbar

Contents Pane

TABLE WIN2.1 Windows Explorer Components

Component	Function
Title bar	Displays the application name and/or the open file name
Menu bar	Provides access to various commands
Standard toolbar	Allows quick access to features
Links toolbar	Offers quick access to various sites on the Internet
Folders pane	Lists the folders and drives to which you have access
Contents pane	Displays the contents of the folder or drive selected in the Folders pane
Status bar	Provides information about the items displayed in the Folders pane and the Contents pane. This information changes depending on what you have selected.

(3) Click the down-pointing triangle at the right side of the Views button on the Windows Explorer Standard toolbar and then click <u>D</u>etails at the drop-list list.

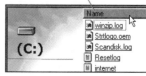

Step 3

Problem

If the Views button is not visible, increase the width of the Windows Explorer window until it displays on the toolbar.

Step 4

If your View is already set to <u>D</u>etails, you can skip step 3.

(4) Click the column heading *Name* to sort the files in descending order.

By default, folder and file names are displayed in ascending order. Clicking the Name column heading changes the order from ascending to descending. Descending order is Z to A for text names and higher numbers to lower numbers for number names written as integers. An integer is a whole number.

(continued)

(5) Click again on the column heading *Name* to sort the files in ascending order.

Ascending order is A to Z for text names and lower numbers to higher numbers for number names written as integers. You can use this sorting technique on all the column headings to switch the sorting order from ascending to descending.

(6) Change the view of the file listing by clicking the down-pointing triangle at the right side of the Views button on the Standard toolbar. The drop-down list includes the following viewing choices: *Large Icons, Small Icons, List*, and *Details*. Refer to Table WIN2.2 for a description of each view.

(7) Click <u>L</u>ist and notice how the display of folders and files changes in the Contents pane.

(8) Click the down-pointing triangle next to the Views button and then click each of the views to see how the view changes.

(9) Return to the <u>L</u>ist view when finished reviewing the options.

(10) Create a new folder on your floppy disk by first inserting a formatted disk in the 3½-inch (Floppy A:) drive.

If your disk is not formatted, see the Take 2 box at the end of this exercise for instructions.

(11) Click *3½ Floppy (A:)* in the Folders pane.

(12) Right-click anywhere in a blank area in the Contents pane.

Right-clicking in the blank area displays a shortcut menu.

(13) At the shortcut menu, point to <u>N</u>ew and then click <u>F</u>older.

Windows creates a new folder icon at the bottom of the Contents pane with the default name *New Folder*. The folder name is automatically selected and an insertion point is positioned at the end of the name.

TABLE WIN2.2 View Options

View	Function
Large Icons	Use this view to display large, easy-to-read icons. You will see only file and folder names.
Small Icons	Use this view to display smaller icons that display in columns. You will see only file and folder names.
List	Use this view to display a columnar list of your files. You will see only file and folder names.
Details	Use this view to see details such as file size and the date and time of creation and modification.

14. With *New Folder* selected, key your last name as the new folder name, and then press Enter.

15. Right-click on the folder you just created.

16. Click Rena<u>m</u>e at the shortcut menu.

    The current folder name is highlighted.

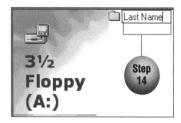

Step 14

17. Key your first name and then press Enter.

18. Delete the folder you just created named with your first name by clicking the Delete button on the Standard toolbar.

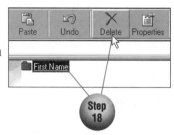

Step 18

19. At the Confirm Folder Delete dialog box, click the <u>Y</u>es button.

20. Click the *(C:)* drive icon in the Folders pane to display the contents of your hard drive.

21. In the Contents pane, locate the folder named *Windows Data Files*, and then click Windows Data Files. (You may need to scroll down the Folders pane to locate the Windows Data Files folder.)

Step 20

    Clicking the folder name opens the folder and displays the names of the files that are stored within the folder in the Contents pane.

22. Right-click on the file in the Contents pane named *Overdue Letter.doc*, and then click <u>C</u>opy at the shortcut menu.

23. Click the *3½ Floppy (A:)* icon in the Folders pane to display the contents of your disk.

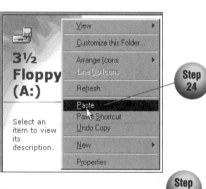

Step 24

24. Right-click in any blank area in the Contents pane and then click <u>P</u>aste at the shortcut menu.

25. Close Windows Explorer by clicking the Close button located in the upper right corner of the window.

Step 25

Formatting a Floppy Disk

Take 2

To format a floppy disk, insert the disk into the drive, and then display Windows Explorer. Right-click on the drive letter in the Folders pane and then click For<u>m</u>at at the shortcut menu. At the Format dialog box, click <u>F</u>ull in the Format type section, and then click the <u>S</u>tart button. Formatting a previously formatted disk erases the disk's contents. If you insert an unformatted disk into the drive and double-click the drive icon, Windows will recognize that the disk is unformatted and offer to format the disk.

Managing Files
Using Windows Explorer

In the previous topic you learned how to create a new folder in Windows Explorer. To further organize your files you can create new folders within existing folders. These folders are sometimes referred to as *subfolders*. For example, assume that you work for a distributing company and you prepare documents that are related to two regions: the NorthWest region and the NorthEast region. Furthermore, in each region, you want to organize your files by the sales activities and the finance activities. You could create two folders: *NorthWest* and *NorthEast*. Within the NorthWest folder you could create two subfolders: *Sales* and *Finance*. Within the NorthEast folder you could also create two folders: *Sales* and *Finance*. Creating subfolders with the same names is possible as long as they are created within different folders at the previous level.

steps

1 Click the Start button on the Taskbar, point to Programs, and then click Windows Explorer.

2 Click *3½ Floppy (A:)* in the Folders pane.

3 If necessary, change to the List view.

> Expand box

4 Right-click in a blank area in the Contents pane, point to New, and then click Folder at the shortcut menu.

5 With *New Folder* selected in the Contents pane, key **NorthWest** and then press Enter.

A plus symbol (+) next to a folder or drive in the Folders pane indicates that the Folders list is currently collapsed and that you are not viewing the entire contents of the disk. Windows Explorer lists folder names in a hierarchical display in the Folders pane. For example, subfolders are displayed as branches off the folders one level above them.

6 Position the tip of the mouse pointer on the plus symbol next to *3½ Floppy (A:)* and then click the left mouse button.

The folder list expands and displays the folder name *NorthWest* below *3½ Floppy (A:)*. When a list has been expanded, the plus symbol changes to a minus symbol. Clicking the minus symbol will collapse the folder list.

> Plus symbol changes to a minus once the folder or disk has been expanded.

7 Click the *NorthWest* folder name in the Folders pane.

The Contents pane will display a blank window since no files or folders currently exist within *NorthWest*. Notice the *NorthWest* folder icon in the Folders pane is now displayed as an open file folder.

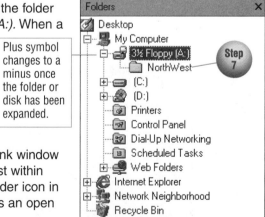

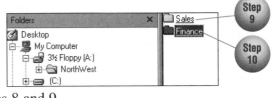
⑧ Right-click in a blank area in the Contents pane, point to <u>N</u>ew, and then click <u>F</u>older at the shortcut menu.

⑨ Key **Sales** as the new folder name and then press Enter.

⑩ Create another new folder within *NorthWest* named Finance by completing steps similar to those in steps 8 and 9.

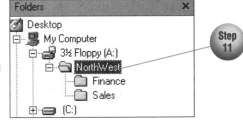

⑪ Click the plus symbol next to the *NorthWest* folder name in the Folders pane to expand the folders list.

The *Finance* and *Sales* folders are listed in alphabetical order below the *NorthWest* folder, which is listed below *3½ Floppy (A:)*. You have created two levels of folders. In the next step you will copy a file from the hard drive to one of the subfolders on the floppy disk.

⑫ Click the *(C:)* icon to display the files and folders in the hard drive in the Contents pane.

⑬ Expand the list of folders in the (C:) drive by clicking the plus symbol.

Skip this step if your list is already expanded.

⑭ Locate and then click the folder named *Windows Data Files* in the Folders pane below *(C:)*. You may need to scroll down the Folders pane to locate the folder.

⑮ Position the pointer over the file named *Sales Budget.xls* (your list may not display the file name extension .xls), hold down the left mouse button, drag the file to the *Sales* subfolder below *NorthWest* in Folders pane, and then release the left mouse button.

Dragging a file name from one drive to another copies the file. This method of copying is referred to as *drag and drop*. To move a file from one drive to another, drag the file name using the *right* mouse button. When you release the mouse, a shortcut menu will appear where you can select *Move Here*.

Problem
?

Can't see the Sales folder in the Folders pane? As you drag the file name toward the top of the pane, the screen will roll upward.

⑯ Click the *Sales* subfolder to display the *Sales Budget.xls* file in the Contents pane.

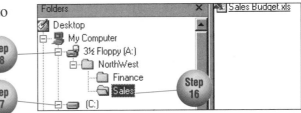

⑰ Click the minus symbol next to *(C:)* to collapse the folder list for the hard drive.

⑱ Click the minus symbol next to *3½ Floppy (A:)* to collapse the folder list for the floppy disk.

⑲ Close the Windows Explorer window.

Deleting and Restoring Files
Using the Recycle Bin

Files you delete are stored in the Recycle Bin until you empty it. These files continue to take up room on your hard drive. You can undelete files that you accidentally deleted, restore folders and shortcuts, and empty the Recycle Bin either one file at a time or all at once. When you undelete a file, you are restoring that file to its previous location. You do not have to remember where the file or folder was originally stored; Windows remembers. Items deleted from a floppy disk or network drive are not stored in the Recycle Bin. If you delete a folder, the Recycle Bin displays the folder icon but does not display the folder contents. However, if you restore the folder, Windows will recreate the folder and all of its contents. Once you have emptied the Recycle Bin, the files are really gone and there is no going back. Some applications use their own delete commands. If you use your program's delete commands, the file may not be placed in the Recycle Bin.

steps

1. At the Windows 98 desktop, click the *My Computer* icon.

2. At the My Computer window, click the *(C:)* drive icon.

3. Click the Windows Data Files folder.

4. Copy a file into the same folder by right-clicking on the file named *Overdue Letter.doc* and then clicking <u>C</u>opy at the shortcut menu.

5. Right-click in a blank area in the window, and then click <u>P</u>aste at the shortcut menu.

   This inserts a new file with the name *Copy of Overdue Letter.doc*.

6. Delete the file you just copied by *right*-clicking the file name and then clicking <u>D</u>elete at the shortcut menu.

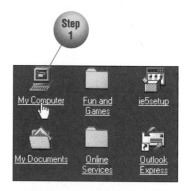

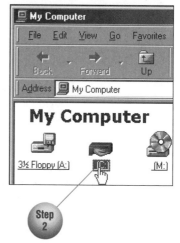

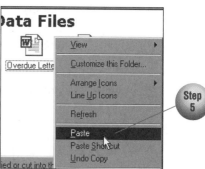

(7) At the Confirm File Delete dialog box, click the <u>Y</u>es button.

Step 7

(8) Close the Windows Data Files window by clicking the Close button located in the upper right corner.

(9) At the Windows 98 desktop, click the *Recycle Bin* icon to open it.

Step 9

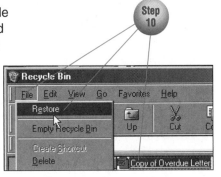

(10) Restore the file you just deleted by pointing to the file name (pointing selects the file name—do not click the mouse button) in the Recycle Bin window. Click <u>F</u>ile on the Menu bar and then click <u>R</u>estore at the drop-down list.

You can also right-click on the file name and then click <u>R</u>estore at the shortcut menu.

(11) Close the Recycle Bin by clicking the Close button located in the upper right corner of the window.

If you want to delete all the files in the Recycle Bin, you would click <u>F</u>ile on the Menu bar and then click Empty Recycle <u>B</u>in. At the Confirm Multiple File Delete dialog box, click the <u>Y</u>es button. Always open the Recycle Bin before emptying it so that you have one last chance to look at the files it contains before they are permanently deleted.

Step 10

Deleting and Restoring Files from Windows Explorer

Take 2

Files can also be deleted and restored in the Recycle Bin from Windows Explorer. At the bottom of the Folders pane is an icon for the Recycle Bin. Click the icon in the Folders pane to view a list of deleted files in the Contents pane. The procedures to delete and restore files from the Recycle Bin in Windows Explorer are the same as what you learned in this topic.

Finding Files

When a disk becomes filled with many files, it can sometimes be too time consuming to scroll through a list of file names in an attempt to locate a particular file. Windows includes the Find feature, which can be used to quickly locate a file on your computer. In addition, files can be located by keying only a portion of the file name in the dialog box. Windows will return a list of all files that meet your search criterion in a separate window. Once the file has been located, you can open it from the Find results window or perform a copy, move, delete, or rename operation on the file.

steps

1. Click the Start button on the Taskbar, point to Find, and then click Files or Folders.

   The Find: All Files dialog box opens.

2. Key *Memo.dot in the Named text box and then click Find Now.

   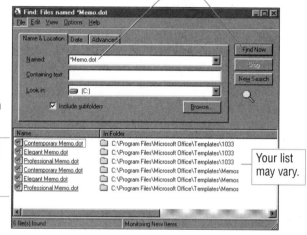

   Step 2

   In a few seconds, Windows will display the list of files that matched your search criterion in the Find Results window. The asterisk in front of Memo.dot indicates to Windows that you want to search for files that have any text in front of Memo.dot in the file name. Notice in the Find results window that the files found begin with a different name but they all end with Memo.dot. The asterisk is referred to as a *wildcard character* and can be inserted in the search criteria in any portion of the name where you do not want to be specific.

   Find results window

   Your list may vary.

Problem?

No files found? Check that the entry in the Look in box is (C:) and that the Include subfolders check box is selected. If not, click the down-pointing triangle next to the Look in box and then click (C:) in the drop-down list and/or click the Include subfolders check box.

3. Select the text in the Named text box and then press the Delete key.

④ Key **Overdue Letter.doc**.

⑤ Click the down-pointing triangle to the right of the <u>L</u>ook in text box and then click *3½ Floppy (A:)* in the drop-down list.

⑥ Click F<u>i</u>nd Now.

In a few seconds the Find results window will display the file named Overdue Letter.doc.

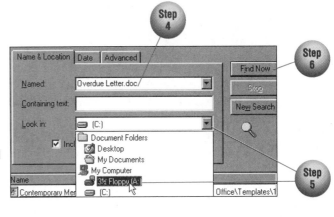

⑦ Right-click Overdue Letter.doc in the Find Results window and then click Rena<u>m</u>e at the shortcut menu.

⑧ Key **Past Due Letter.doc** and then press Enter.

⑨ Click the down-pointing triangle next to the <u>L</u>ook in text box and then click (C:) in the drop-down list.

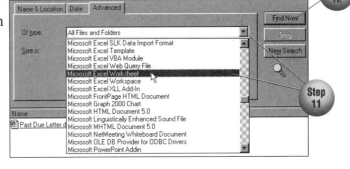

⑩ Click the Advanced tab in the Find dialog box.

You can search for files based on the type of file instead of the file name. In the next step you will specify that you want to search for all Microsoft Excel worksheet files stored on the (C:) drive.

⑪ Click the down-pointing triangle to the right of the Of <u>t</u>ype text box, scroll down the list of file types until you see *Microsoft Excel Worksheet* and then click to select it.

⑫ Click F<u>i</u>nd Now.

In a few seconds all of the Excel worksheet files stored on the hard drive will appear in the Find results window.

⑬ Close the Find Files of type Microsoft Excel Worksheet dialog box.

Finding Files in Windows Explorer

The Find feature is located on the <u>T</u>ools menu in Windows Explorer. To open the Find: All Files dialog box from Windows Explorer, click <u>T</u>ools, point to <u>F</u>ind, and then click <u>F</u>iles or Folders. The Find feature that is available in Windows Explorer is the same feature discussed in this topic.

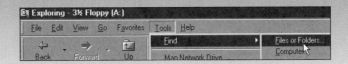

Opening Files from Different Applications

Windows allows you to have more than one file and program open at the same time. The number of files and programs you can open depends on your system memory. Each time a program is installed on your computer, it writes certain information about itself into a special area of Windows called the Registry. Part of the information it gives Windows is what type of extension it uses to identify its files. An extension is the part of the file name that follows the period. For example, each of the following file names ends with an extension that is associated with a particular program:

File Name and Extension	Application that is Associated with the File
Overdue Letter.doc	Microsoft Word
Sales Budget.xls	Microsoft Excel
Customers.mdb	Microsoft Access
Employee Orientation.ppt	Microsoft PowerPoint

Two files can have exactly the same name as long as they have different extensions. When you click a file name in either Windows Explorer or the My Computer window, Windows looks at the extension and determines the program in which to open the file.

steps

1 Click the *My Computer* icon on the desktop.

This displays the My Computer window as shown in Figure WIN2.2. Your My Computer window may vary slightly from what you see in the figure.

FIGURE WIN2.2 My Computer Window

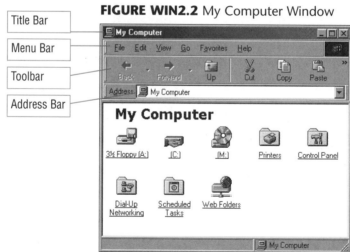

2 Click the *(C:)* drive icon.

3 Click the *Windows Data Files* folder to open it.

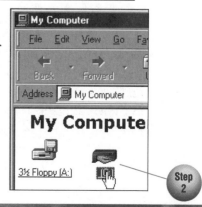

Step 2

(4) Click the file named *Overdue Letter.doc*. Notice that the file opens in Microsoft Word.

Problem

?

If you get an error message when attempting to open a file, the application in which the document was created may not have been installed on your computer. Check with your instructor.

Step 4

(5) Click the Windows Data Files button on the Taskbar to return to the Windows Data Files window.

(6) Click the file named *Sales Budget.xls*. Notice that the file opens in Microsoft Excel.

(7) Click the Windows Data Files button on the Taskbar to return to the Windows Data Files window.

(8) Click the file named *Customers.mdb*. Notice that the file opens in Microsoft Access.

(9) Click the Windows Data Files button on the Taskbar to return to the Windows Data Files window.

(10) Click the file named *Employee Orientation.ppt*. Notice that the file opens in Microsoft PowerPoint.

(11) Close the *Overdue Letter.doc* file by right-clicking on the file name on the Taskbar and then clicking Close at the pop-up menu. (If prompted to save changes, click the No button.)

Step 11

(12) Complete steps similar to those in 11 to close the other three files and also the Windows Data Files window. (You should be returned to the Windows 98 desktop.)

You can move back and forth between the different files by clicking the file name button on the Taskbar.

Opening Unassociated Files

Take **2**

A file that has been named with a file extension that Windows does not recognize will cause the Open With dialog box to appear when you click the file name. Scroll through the list of software application programs in the Choose the program you want to use list box and then double-click the application in which you want the file opened.

Browsing Disks and Devices Using My Computer

My Computer allows you to browse the contents of your hard disk, network drives, and floppy drives; and you can open files from the My Computer window. You can add network or local printers, create Web folders, configure dial-up networking, schedule computer maintenance tasks such as scan disk and disk defragmenter, and access the Control Panel. Scan Disk is a utility program that checks your hard drive for errors and offers to correct the errors. Disk defragmenter is a utility that optimizes hard drive space by reorganizing file clusters so that programs open faster and files take up less space. The Control Panel allows you to customize the appearance of all aspects of the Windows environment. You can also add and remove programs from your computer using the Control Panel. At the top of the My Computer window is a toolbar that allows you to navigate backward and forward to your previous locations.

steps

1. Click the *My Computer* icon to display all the drives to which you currently have access.

2. Click the *Printers* icon.

   Clicking the Printers icon displays a list of printers to which you are connected or that you can access. You can add a new printer by clicking the *Add Printer* icon.

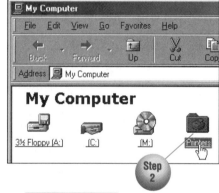

3. Click the Back button on the toolbar to return to the My Computer window.

Back button not active? Click View in the My Computer menu bar and then click Folder Options. Click Web style in the Windows Desktop Update section and then click OK.

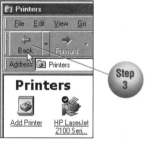

4. Click the *Control Panel* icon.

   The Control Panel window displays a list of options that help you configure and customize various aspects of Windows.

5. Review the list of icons in the Control Panel window to see the available options with which you can customize in the Windows environment.

   Clicking an icon will open a window or dialog box where the settings can be modified.

6. Click the Back button on the toolbar to return to the My Computer window.

7 Click the *Dial-Up Networking* icon.

Clicking this icon starts a wizard that will walk you through establishing a dial-up connection to the Internet or to another network.

Problem

?

If a dial-up connection has already been established on the computer you are using, the window will display an icon for the existing dial-up connection and another icon named *Make New Connection*. Click Make New Connection to start the wizard for step 7.

8 Click the Cancel button to remove the Welcome to Dial-Up Networking or Make New Connection dialog box.

9 Click the Back button on the toolbar to return to the My Computer window.

10 Click the *Scheduled Tasks* icon.

This feature allows you to set up certain disk maintenance and other types of tasks to be performed at regular intervals. The Scheduled Tasks wizard is included to walk you through the necessary steps.

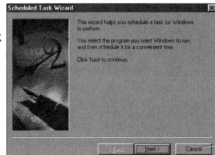

11 Click *Add Scheduled Task* in the Scheduled Tasks window.

This will start the Scheduled Task Wizard.

Step 12

12 Click the Cancel button to remove the Scheduled Task Wizard dialog box.

13 Click the Back button on the toolbar to return to the My Computer window.

14 Click the *Web Folders* icon in the My Computer window.

Open Web Folders to create shortcuts to your company's Intranet or Internet sites. Click the *Add Web Folder* icon to start the Add Web Folder wizard.

Click to start the Add Web Folder Wizard.

15 Click the Back button on the toolbar to return to the My Computer window.

16 Close the My Computer window.

Take 2

Modifying Tasks Schedules

Once scheduled tasks are created, you can modify the program or the schedule. To do this, open the Scheduled Tasks window, right-click the task, and then click Properties at the shortcut menu. Change the settings as required. If a scheduled task is no longer needed, it can be deleted from the Scheduled Tasks window by right-clicking the task and then clicking Delete at the shortcut menu. If a task begins while you are working on the computer, you can stop the task and restart it later. To do this, right-click the task in the Scheduled Tasks window and then click End Task at the shortcut menu. To restart the task later, right-click the task and then click Run.

Customizing the Desktop

The desktop is the area of Windows that you see when you first start your computer. It has characteristics of a conventional desktop, including the ability to move your work around and rearrange items to suit your working style. Changing the desktop wallpaper (the background) gives Windows a whole new look. You can also add a *screen saver* to protect your monitor from burn-in and to give you added security. A screen saver is a utility that causes the screen to blank out or display a certain image after a specified period of time. Other elements that can be changed include the color scheme and the arrangement of icons on the desktop. If you work with a program frequently, you may find it easier to create a shortcut to that program and place it on your desktop. Setting the system date and time is another helpful skill to know.

steps

1. Right-click an empty area of the desktop (do not right-click an icon).

2. Click Properties at the shortcut menu.

3. At the Display Properties dialog box with the Background tab selected, scroll through the choices in the Wallpaper section and then click a wallpaper style.

   When you click a wallpaper style, a preview of the wallpaper displays in the monitor image in the dialog box.

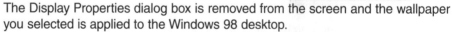

4. Click the OK button.

   The Display Properties dialog box is removed from the screen and the wallpaper you selected is applied to the Windows 98 desktop.

5. Right-click an empty area of the desktop and then click Properties at the shortcut menu.

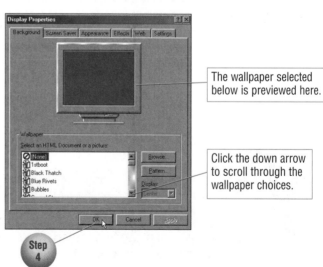

The wallpaper selected below is previewed here.

Click the down arrow to scroll through the wallpaper choices.

Step 2

Step 4

6 At the Display Properties dialog box, click the Screen Saver tab.

7 Click the down-pointing triangle at the right of the Screen Saver name box to display a list of available screen savers.

8 Click one of the screen saver names in the drop-down list.

9 Select the current number in the Wait text box and then key **1**.

With the **1** entered in the Wait text box, the selected screen saver will display on your screen after one minute of no movement on the screen.

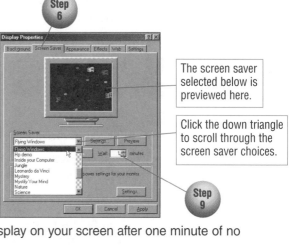

Step 6

The screen saver selected below is previewed here.

Click the down triangle to scroll through the screen saver choices.

Step 9

10 Click the Appearance tab in the Display Properties dialog box.

11 Click the down-pointing triangle at the right of the Scheme name box and then click one of the schemes in the drop-down list.

You will see a preview of the scheme in the display window.

12 Click OK to close the dialog box and apply your choices.

Click the Cancel button if you do not want to apply your choices.

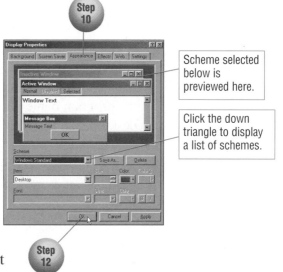

Step 10

Scheme selected below is previewed here.

Click the down triangle to display a list of schemes.

Step 12

13 Right-click an empty area of the desktop, point to Arrange Icons at the shortcut menu, and then click By Name in the side menu.

Your icons are arranged alphabetically from top to bottom. Icons that are a part of the Windows installation are always listed first.

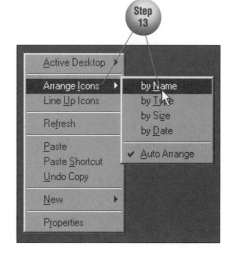

Step 13

(continued)

14 Right-click an empty area of the desktop, point to Arrange Icons at the shortcut menu, and then click Auto Arrange to remove the check mark.

Skip this step if Auto Arrange displays without a check mark.

15 Drag the *Recycle Bin* icon to the lower right corner of your screen.

16 Drag the other icons on your screen to arrange them in a circle.

17 Right-click an empty area of the desktop, point to Arrange Icons, and then click Auto Arrange.

This turns on the Auto Arrange feature and all the icons snap back to the left side of the screen.

18 Try to move an icon with Auto Arrange turned on.

When Auto Arrange is turned on, you can only exchange icons between locations. You cannot move an icon to a new location.

19 To create a shortcut to the Paint program, click the Start button on the Taskbar, point to Programs, point to Accessories, and then point to Paint. (Do not click Paint.)

20 With the mouse pointer pointing to Paint, hold down the *right* mouse button, drag the program name onto the desktop, and then release the mouse button.

21 At the shortcut menu that displays, click Create Shortcut(s) Here.

The Paint icon displays on your desktop with the shortcut arrow in the bottom left corner.

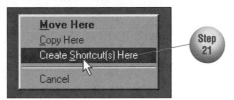

22 Remove the Paint shortcut icon by positioning the mouse pointer on the icon, clicking the *right* mouse button, and then clicking <u>D</u>elete at the shortcut menu.

23 At the Confirm File Delete dialog box, click the <u>Y</u>es button.

24 Double-click the time located at the right side of the Taskbar.

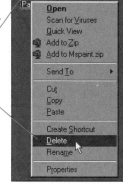

Step 22

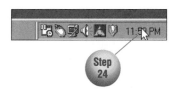

Step 24

25 At the Date/Time Properties dialog box, check to make sure the correct month, day, and time display in the dialog box. If necessary, make corrections to the month, day, or time options.

26 Click OK to close the Date/Time Properties dialog box.

27 Check with your instructor to see if you should restore the desktop to the original settings.

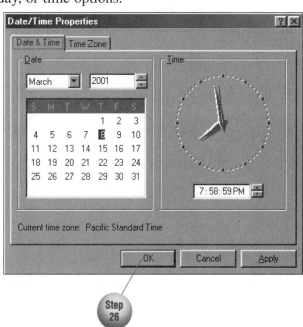

Step 26

Setting a Screen Saver Password

To add a security level to your computer, consider setting a password on your screen saver. Open the Display Properties dialog box with the Screen Saver tab selected and click in the <u>P</u>assword protected check box. Key a password that must be entered before the screen saver will be deactivated. Click the <u>C</u>hange button and enter the password twice for verification. If you forget your password, you will not be able to deactivate the screen saver.

Take 2

Customizing the Start Menu and Saving a Scheme

By default, the Start menu displays with large icons next to the menu item name and the Windows 98 banner running along the left side. You can modify the appearance of the Start menu to suit your preferences. You can change the size of the icons and add and delete items to the menu. The font and font color of window elements can be modified at the Display Properties dialog box. Once the Start menu and desktop look exactly the way you want, you can save the appearance scheme.

steps

1. Click the Start button on the Taskbar and then point to Settings.

2. Click Taskbar & Start Menu.

   This causes the Taskbar Properties dialog box to open.

3. Click the Show small icons in Start menu check box.

4. Click OK.

   The Start menu will now display small icons.

5. Right-click in an empty area of the desktop.

6. Click Properties at the shortcut menu and then click the Appearance tab.

7. Click the Title bar labeled *Active Window* in the preview area of the dialog box.

   This will activate the Item and Font options at the bottom of the dialog box.

8. Click the down-pointing triangle at the right of the Font name box and then click one of the font names in the pop-up list.

9. Click the down-pointing triangle to the right of the Color box in the Active Title Bar section and then click one of the color boxes in the color palette.

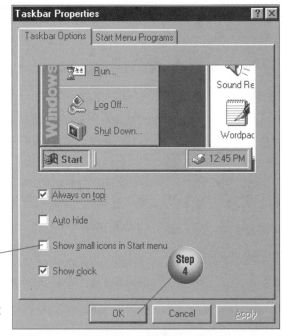

In steps 10 through 12 you will learn how to change the size of the icons on the Desktop.

10 Click the down-pointing triangle to the right of the Item name box (currently reads *Active Title Bar*) and then click *Icon* in the drop-down list.

11 Click the up- or down-pointing triangle to the right of the Size text box until the size is 40.

The default size is 32. Choose a larger number to increase the size of the icons or a smaller number to decrease their size.

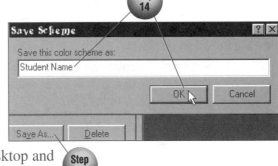

12 Click the Apply button.

In a few seconds the current settings will be applied to the Desktop. If necessary, drag the Display Properties dialog box to the side of the screen to view the new settings. The current settings can be saved as a *scheme* that can be restored at any time by clicking the scheme name in the Scheme drop-down list.

13 Click the Save As button to the right of the Scheme name box.

14 Key your first and last name in the Save Scheme dialog box and then click OK.

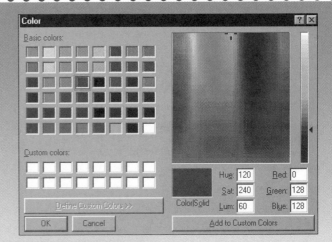

15 Click OK to close the Display Properties dialog box.

16 Check with your instructor to see if you should restore the desktop and Start menu to the original settings.

Problem

Can't remember the original settings? Change the Scheme to Windows Standard. This will restore the scheme to the default scheme used when Windows 98 was installed.

Additional Color Options

Although the Appearance tab in the Properties dialog box offers several color choices for menu items, even more color options are available. If you do not see the color you want in the Color palette, click the button labeled Other. This opens the Color dialog box shown at the right, where you can create a custom color.

Using Paint and WordPad

Windows 98 includes accessory programs such as Paint, Calculator, and WordPad, which are simple, easy-to-use applications. Paint is a program that can be used to create and modify simple images. Use Calculator to perform the mathematical functions offered on calculators and then paste your results into another Windows application. WordPad is a word processing program that offers some of the features of Microsoft Word but is not as comprehensive. Some other accessories included in Windows are Notepad, a text editor program that allows you to create and modify text files; and Address Book, a personal data application that allows you to keep track of your addresses and other contact information.

steps

1. Click the Start button on the Taskbar, point to Programs, point to Accessories, and then click Paint.

   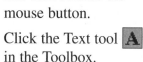

   This opens the Paint application as shown in Figure WIN2.3. An image is created in Paint by clicking a tool in the toolbox. Position the pointer in the Drawing area and then drag the pointer to create a shape.

   FIGURE WIN2.3 Paint Window

   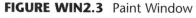
   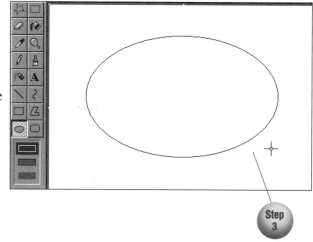

2. Click the Ellipse tool ⬭ in the Toolbox.

3. Position the pointer in the top left of the drawing area, hold down the left mouse button, drag down and to the right to create an oval the approximate height and width shown at the right, and then release the mouse button.

   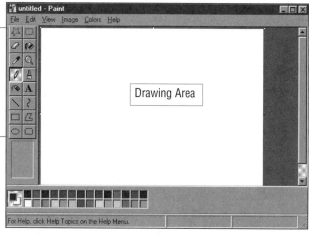

   Step 3

4. Click the Text tool **A** in the Toolbox.

5 Position the pointer at the top left inside the oval, hold down the left mouse button, drag the pointer down and to the right to create a dashed border the approximate height and width shown at the right, and then release the mouse button.

An insertion point will appear inside the dashed rectangular border when you release the mouse button.

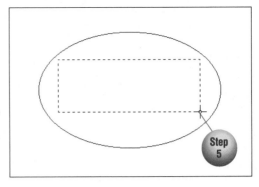

Step 5

6 Key your first and last name inside the text box.

7 Print the image by clicking <u>F</u>ile and then <u>P</u>rint. At the Print dialog box, click OK.

8 Experiment with some of the other buttons in the Toolbox and the Color palette at the bottom of the Paint window.

To discard the current drawing and start a new image, click <u>F</u>ile and then <u>N</u>ew. Click <u>N</u>o when prompted to save changes to the current image.

9 Close the Paint window. Click <u>N</u>o when prompted to save changes.

10 Click the Start button on the Taskbar, point to <u>P</u>rograms, point to Accessories, and then click WordPad.

This opens the WordPad application as shown in Figure WIN2.4. WordPad is a word processing program, which is suitable for keying simple letters and memos. It does not contain all of the features of a full-fledged word processing program such as Microsoft Word.

FIGURE WIN2.4 WordPad Window

11 With the insertion point blinking in the top left corner of the Document area, key the current date and then press the Enter key twice to move down a double-space on the page.

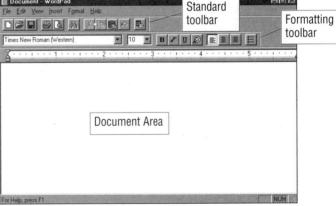

12 Key the following paragraph of text. Do not press the Enter key when you reach the edge of the window. WordPad will automatically wrap the text to the next line.

Windows accessory programs are simple and easy to use. The Paint program is a graphics application that can be used to create drawings. WordPad is a word processor that can be used to type letters or memos.

13 Press the Enter key twice to create a blank line at the end of the text and then key your first and last name.

14 Click the Print button on the Standard toolbar.

15 Close the WordPad window. Click <u>N</u>o when prompted to save changes.

Exploring the Windows Help Feature

Windows 98 includes an on-screen reference guide providing information, explanations, and interactive help on learning Windows features. The on-screen reference guide, referred to as "Help," contains complex files with hypertext used to access additional information by clicking a word or phrase. The Help feature can interact with open programs to help guide you through difficult tasks. If you have Internet access, you can get direct help from the Microsoft Web site. Display the Windows Help window by clicking the Start button and then clicking Help at the pop-up menu. The Windows Help window contains three tabs: Contents, Index, and Search. Click the tab that provides the Help options you need to find the desired information.

steps

1. Click the Start button on the Taskbar and then click Help at the pop-up menu.

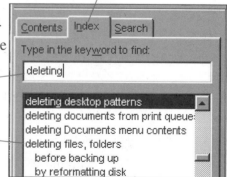

2. At the Windows Help dialog box, click the Contents tab.

   Skip this step if the Contents tab is already selected.

3. Learn about basic Windows 98 features by clicking *Introducing Windows 98* in the list box.

   The book icon preceding *Introducing Windows 98* displays as an open book and a list of topics display below it.

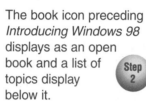

4. Click *What's New in Windows 98*.

   The book icon preceding *What's New in Windows 98* displays as an open book and a list of topics displays below it with each item preceded by a question mark icon.

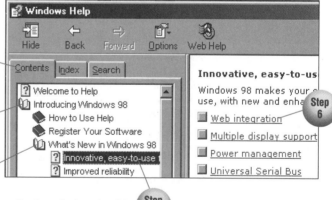

5. Click *Innovative, easy-to-use features*.

   A list of topics appears in the help box at the right side of the Windows Help window.

6. Click *Web integration* and then read the information that displays in the help box.

7. Click the Index tab.

8. With the insertion point positioned in the top text box, key **deleting**.

⑨ Double-click *deleting files, folders* in the list box.

⑩ At the Topics Found dialog box, click *To delete a file or folder* in the list box, click the Display button, and then read the information that displays in the Windows Help box.

Step 11

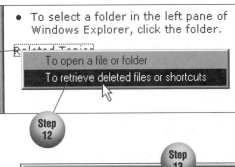

• To select a folder in the left pane of Windows Explorer, click the folder.

To open a file or folder
To retrieve deleted files or shortcuts

Step 12

⑪ Click Related Topics at the bottom of the Windows Help box.

⑫ At the list that displays, click *To retrieve deleted files or shortcuts*, and then read the information that displays in the Windows Help box.

⑬ Click the Search tab.

⑭ Key **online** in the first text box and then click the List Topics button.

Help displays a list of topics that include the word "online."

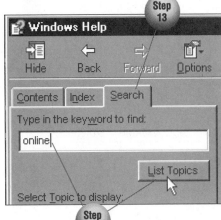

Step 13

Windows Help

Hide   Back   Forward   Options

Contents | Index | Search

Type in the keyword to find:

online

List Topics

Select Topic to display:

Step 14

⑮ Double-click *Connecting to the Internet* in the Select Topic to display list box.

⑯ Print the information by clicking the Options button on the Toolbar and then clicking Print at the drop-down list. At the Print dialog box, click the OK button.

⑰ Close the Windows Help window by clicking the Close button located in the upper right corner of the window.

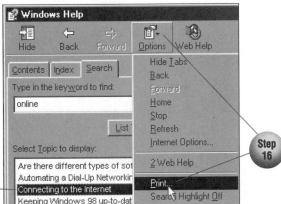

Windows Help

Hide   Back   Forward   Options   Web Help

Contents | Index | Search

Type in the keyword to find:

online

List

Select Topic to display:

Are there different types of sof
Automating a Dial-Up Networkir
Connecting to the Internet
Keeping Windows 98 up-to-dat

Hide Tabs
Back
Forward
Home
Stop
Refresh
Internet Options...

2 Web Help

Print...
Search Highlight Off

Step 15

Step 16

Take 2

Windows Help Toolbar Buttons

Use the buttons on the Windows Help toolbar to perform the following actions:

Button	Action
Hide	Hide the table of contents, index, or search results. When you click this button it changes to the Show button.
Back	Display last Help topic you saw.
Forward	Display the next Help topic in a previously displayed sequence of topics.
Options	Display a drop-down list for options for working with the Help feature including hiding tabs, moving backward or forward through Help topics, displaying the home page, stopping the loading of a page, refreshing a previously opened page, displaying Internet options, and printing the current topic.
Web Help	Connect to the Microsoft Support Online site.

Features Summary

In Windows Explorer Feature	Button	Action
Open Windows Explorer		Start, Programs, Windows Explorer
Create new folder		Right-click Contents pane, point to New, click Folder
Rename folder		Right-click folder, click Rename, key new name
Delete folder	☒	Right-click folder, click Delete
Copy file		Right-click file, click Copy
Expand folder	⊞	
Collapse folder	⊟	
Close Windows Explorer	☒	File, Close

In My Computer Feature	Button	Action
Display My Computer window		Click My Computer icon
Copy a file	📄	Right-click file, click Copy
Delete a file	☒	Right-click file, click Delete
Display previous window	⇦	
Close My Computer window	☒	File, Close

In Recycle Bin Feature	Button	Action
Display Recycle Bin		Click Recycle Bin icon
Restore file		File, Restore or right-click file, click Restore
Close Recycle Bin	☒	File, Close

Specific Features Feature	Button	Action
Display Find: All Files dialog box		Start, Find, Files or Folders
Display Properties dialog box		Right-click empty area of desktop, click Properties
Arrange desktop icons		Right click empty area of desktop, point to Arrange Icons, click desired arrangement
Create a shortcut		Point to program, hold down right mouse drag onto desktop, release button
Display Date/Time Properties dialog box		Double-click time located in Status bar
Display Taskbar Properties dialog box		Start, Settings, Taskbar & Start Menu
Display Paint program		Start, Programs, Accessories, Paint
Display WordPad program		Start, Programs, Accessories, WordPad
Display Windows Help window		Start, Help

Procedures Check

Look at the Windows Explorer window shown above. This screen contains numbers with lines pointing to specific items. Write the name of the item after the number below that corresponds with the number in the window.

1. _____
2. _____
3. _____

4. _____
5. _____
6. _____

In the space provided, write the steps you would complete to display the following window, dialog box, or program.

7. Windows Explorer window _____
8. My Computer window _____
9. Find: All Files dialog box _____
10. Properties dialog box _____
11. Taskbar Properties dialog box _____
12. WordPad program _____
13. Paint program _____
14. Windows Help window _____

In the space provided, write the steps you would complete to accomplish the following tasks.

15. Create a new folder in Windows Explorer

_____

16. Expand a folder in Windows Explorer

_____

17. Delete a file from the My Computer window

_____

18. Restore a file from the Recycle Bin

_____

Skills Review

Activity 1: Creating Folders; Copying Files with Windows Explorer

1   Open Windows Explorer.
2   Click *3½ Floppy (A:)* in the Folders pane.
3   Create a new folder and name it NorthEast.
4   Expand the folders list for 3½ Floppy (A:).
5   Click *NorthEast* in the Folders pane.
6   Create two subfolders within the NorthEast folder and name them as follows:
      Sales
      Finance
7   Expand the folders list for NorthEast.
8   Click *(C:)* in the Folders pane.
9   If necessary, expand the folders list for (C:).
10 Click the folder named *Windows Data Files*.
11 Copy the file named Customers.mdb from Windows Data Files to the Sales subfolder within NorthEast on the floppy disk.
12 Copy the file named Employee Orientation.ppt from Windows Data Files to the Finance subfolder within NorthEast on the floppy disk.
13 Collapse the folder list for (C:).
14 Collapse the folder list for 3½ Floppy (A:).
15 Close Windows Explorer.

Activity 2: Renaming and Deleting Files

1   Open Windows Explorer.
2   Expand the folders list for 3½ Floppy (A:) and then expand the folder list for the NorthEast folder.
3   Display the contents of the Sales subfolder within the NorthEast folder.

4 Rename Customers.mdb to NorthEast.mdb.
5 Display the contents of the Finance subfolder within the NorthEast folder.
6 Delete the file named Employee Orientation.ppt.
7 Collapse the NorthEast folders list.
8 Expand the folders list for the NorthWest folder.
9 Display the contents of the Sales subfolder within the NorthWest folder.
10 Rename Sales Budget.xls to NorthWest Sales.xls.
11 Collapse the NorthWest folders list.
12 Collapse the 3½ Floppy (A:) folders list.
13 Close Windows Explorer.

Activity 3: Finding Files

1 Open the Find: All Files dialog box.
2 Key **letter** in the Named text box in the Name & Location tab. The asterisk before and after *letter* indicates that the files found can start with any text, then contain the text *letter*, and then end with any other text.
3 Check the following settings and change the options if necessary:
   Look in   (C:)
   Include subfolders   selected
4 Click the Advanced tab.
5 Make sure All Files and Folders is selected in the Of type text box.
6 Click the Date tab.
7 Make sure All files is selected.
8 Click Find Now.
9 Review the search results to see the pattern in the list of files found (see step 2).
10 Close the Find dialog box.

Activity 4: Customizing the Desktop

1 Right-click in an empty area of the desktop.
2 Click Properties at the shortcut menu.
3 If necessary, click the Background tab.
4 Write down the current wallpaper name.
   _____
5 Change the wallpaper to *Carved Stone*.
6 Click the down-pointing triangle to the right of the Display text box and then click *Stretch* in the drop-down list. (Skip this step if Display is already set to *Stretch*.)
7 Click Apply.
8 Click the Appearance tab.
9 Write down the current scheme name.
   _____
10 Change the Scheme to *Rose*.
11 Click OK.
12 Restore the Display Properties to their original settings. (See the text you wrote for steps 4 and 9.)

Activity 5: Creating a Document in WordPad

1 Open WordPad.
2 Key the following text. Use the Tab key to align the text at the second column. *(Hint: In some cases you may need to press the Tab key more than once to align the second column text.)*

Accessory:	**Used For:**
Address Book	**Maintain a list of names and addresses**
Calculator	**Perform mathematical computations**
NotePad	**View or key a small amount of text such as a note**
WordPad	**View or key text. Some formatting options are available**

3 Make sure your floppy disk is in the disk drive.
4 Click File and then click Save.
5 Key **Accessories** in the File name text box.
6 Click the down-pointing triangle to the right of the Save in text box and then click *3½ Floppy (A:)* in the drop-down list.
7 Click the Save button located in the bottom right corner of the Save As dialog box.
8 Click the Print button on the toolbar.
9 Exit WordPad.

Performance Plus

Activity 1: Organizing Files and Folders Using Windows Explorer

1 After learning how to create folders and subfolders you have decided to reorganize the way you store files to conform to the following structure:

- 3½ Floppy (A:)
  - Letters
    - Customers
    - Suppliers
  - Budgets
    - Sales
    - Administration
  - Miscellaneous

2 Open Windows Explorer.
3 With your floppy disk inserted in the disk drive, right-click 3½ Floppy (A:) and then click Format at the shortcut menu.
4 Click Full in the Format type section in the Format - 3½ Floppy (A:) dialog box and then click Start. The formatting process will take a few minutes to complete. When the format is complete, click the Close button in the Format Results - 3½ Floppy (A:) dialog box. Click the Close button in the Format - 3½ Floppy (A:) dialog box.
5 Create the folders according to the structure shown in step 1.

6 Display the contents of the Windows Data Files folder on the hard drive and then copy the following files to the designated folders on the floppy disk.

Copy To	Folder/Subfolder
Overdue Letter.doc	Customers
Sales Budget.xls	Sales
Customers.mdb	Miscellaneous
Employee Orientation.ppt	Miscellaneous

7 Close Windows Explorer.

Activity 2: Deleting and Restoring Files

1 Use the My Computer window to display the contents of the Windows Data Files folder on the hard drive.
2 Delete all of the files within the folder.
3 Minimize the Windows Data Files window.
4 Open the Recycle Bin.
5 Restore the files that were deleted in step 2.
6 Close the Recycle Bin.
7 Restore the Windows Data Files window to verify that the files have been restored to their original location.
8 Close the Windows Data Files window.

Activity 3: Customizing the Desktop

1 After learning how to customize the desktop to suit your preferences you decide to make the following changes:
   • Create a shortcut on the desktop to open Windows Explorer
   • Change the screen saver and wallpaper
   • Decrease the size of the icons
2 Write down the current settings on the computer you are using for the following options:
   Screen saver _____
   Wallpaper _____
   Scheme _____
   Icon size _____
3 Create the shortcut on the desktop to Windows Explorer.
4 Open the Display Properties dialog box and change the screen saver, wallpaper, and icon size to a setting of your choice.
5 Save the current settings as a new scheme. Name the scheme xxScheme where xx is your first and last initials.
6 Restore the desktop to the original settings you noted in step 2.

Activity 4: Creating an Image in Paint

1 Open Paint.
2 Look at Figure WIN2.5. This image was created in Paint by overlapping objects. The text box overlaps the oval, which overlaps the rectangle.
3 Create the figure shown in Figure WIN2.5 to the best of your ability. Use the help in Paint to determine how to change the colors of the objects.
4 Save the image on your floppy disk and name it Sale Sign.
5 Print the image.
6 Exit Paint.

FIGURE WIN2.5

Sale Starts Today!

Activity 5: Finding Information on the Active Desktop

1 Use the Windows online help to find information on the Active Desktop. In particular, look for information on what the active desktop is and how to use it.
2 Open WordPad.
3 Compose a memo to your instructor providing a brief synopsis of the information you learned in the help. Include the current date and your name in the memo.
4 Save the memo on your floppy disk and name it Active Desktop Memo.
5 Print the memo.
6 Exit WordPad.

Activity 6: Finding Support Information for Windows 98 Online

1 Make sure you are connected to the Internet.
2 Click the Start button on the Taskbar and then click Help.
3 At the Windows Help window, click the Web Help button on the toolbar.
4 Scroll down the list box at the right side of the Windows Help window until you see the text *Support Online* and then click *Support Online*.
5 When the Microsoft Personal Online Support page displays, click *Using Windows 98* that displays at the left side of the screen below the heading *Using....*
6 At the Windows 98 window, click a topic that interests you. Continue clicking interesting hyperlinks until you display information about a specific topic.
7 Click the Print button to print the topic.
8 Click the Close button located in the upper right corner of the window to close your browser.

Activity 7: Deleting the Shortcut and Scheme

1 Delete the shortcut to the Windows Explorer you created in Performance Plus Activity 3, step 3.
2 Delete the scheme you created in Performance Plus Activity 3, step 5. *(Hint: Use the online Help if you are not sure how to delete a scheme.)*
3 Delete the scheme you saved in steps 13-14 on page 37.

Windows® 98
Navigating the Internet with Internet Explorer

In companies across the nation, employees quickly and easily exchange information through the company intranet. From homes and businesses around the world, people are communicating with one another and accessing astonishing amounts of information through the Internet. Computer networks enable this easy access to people and information.

A computer *network* is a group of computers and other hardware devices that are linked through telecommunications systems so that applications, data, and messages can be shared. The Internet is the largest network of them all, connecting more than 35,000 other networks, which, in turn, connect approximately 25 million computers in 92 countries.

The Internet began as a Defense Department network that was created to allow scientists, engineers, and academic and military researchers to exchange research and to access the same data. In 1969, the United States government funded an experimental network called ARPAnet, or the network for the Advanced Research Projects Agency. The system eventually linked universities, government facilities, and corporations around the world. ARPAnet is the precursor of today's Internet.

Perhaps the most popular part of the Internet is the World Wide Web. The World Wide Web is a collection of hypertext documents, or Web pages, that you can navigate using hyperlinks. A *hyperlink* is a coded location represented by underlined text or a graphic within a document that, when clicked, jumps the user to related information. To navigate the World Wide Web, you need a piece of software called a Web *browser*. Windows 98 includes a Web browser called Internet Explorer 5.0. Web browsers allow you to access a Web site, display text and graphics, and follow hyperlinks.

Web browsers such as Internet Explorer are also used to navigate company intranets. An *intranet* is a private collection of networks, often found within a corporation, that uses a Web browser and other services similar to those provided by the Internet to access internal information. Whereas the Internet is a collection of public networks, an intranet is a collection of private or internal networks. Think of an intranet as a mini-Internet within a company.

Internet Explorer is a useful tool for navigating the Internet or a company intranet. In this section, you will learn the following Explorer skills.

Skills

- Start Internet Explorer and identify parts of the window
- Navigate the World Wide Web
- Add a Web page to the Favorites list and organize the list
- Search the Web
- Review Web channels
- Copy and save text, graphics, and sound
- Work offline
- Work with hypermedia

Starting and Closing Internet Explorer 5 and Identifying Parts of the Window

To access the Internet, you must have an Internet service provider, or ISP. An ISP is a company that offers Internet access to subscribers for a small monthly fee. Subscribers are provided a local telephone number that connects them to the ISP's Internet access point. The ISP leases phone lines that provide a direct connection to the Internet. Once you are connected to the Internet through your ISP, you can access Internet Explorer in one of several ways: 1) the Internet Explorer option on the Start menu; 2) the Internet Explorer shortcut on the Quick Launch toolbar to the right of the Start button; and 3) the Internet Explorer icon that is automatically added to the desktop when Windows 98 is installed. When Explorer is started, it displays the *home page*. The home page refers not only to the page that is displayed when a browser is first opened, but also to the first or top-level page of any Web site. You can choose any Web page to be the first page displayed when Internet Explorer is opened. Usually, the home page contains links to the other pages on the site. It may also contain links to other sites.

steps

Before you begin, check with your instructor about how to connect to your Internet Service Provider.

1. Connect to your Internet Service Provider. Then click the Explorer icon .

   Once Internet Explorer starts, your screen will look similar to the screen in Figure Win3.1, in which the home page for the Microsoft Network is displayed.

Problem?

If a sign-in screen appears asking for a user name and a password, check with either your instructor or lab assistant for the proper sign-in and password.

FIGURE WIN3.1 Microsoft Network Home Page

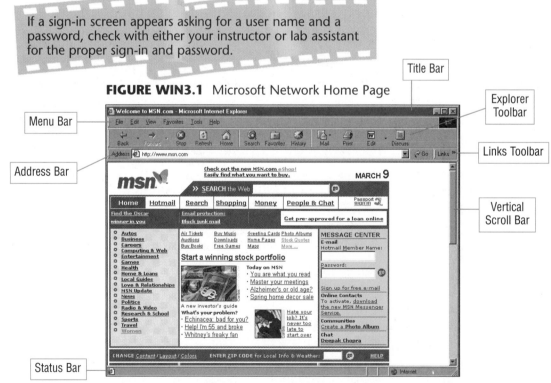

2. Position the mouse pointer on the Title bar at the top of the screen.

   Whatever is displayed in the Title bar is the name of that particular Web page.

3 Move the mouse pointer to the Menu bar and notice that it has the following pull-down menus: File, Edit, View, Favorites, Tools, Help.

4 Move the mouse pointer to the Explorer toolbar shown below. Move your mouse over the following buttons, pausing on each one: Back, Forward, Stop, Refresh, Home, Search, Favorites, History, Mail, Print, Edit.

The functions of the buttons on the Explorer toolbar are explained in Table WIN3.1

TABLE WIN3.1 Explorer Toolbar Buttons

Button	Function
Back	Returns the user to the previous page
Forward	Takes the user to the next page in a series of pages that were already visited
Stop	Stops the downloading of a page
Refresh	Updates the current page if all the latest or expected information did not appear
Home	Takes the user to the home page (the first page displayed when the browser is opened)
Search	Opens the Search bar, from which the user can choose a search service and search the Internet
Favorites	Opens the Favorites bar, which stores links (shortcuts) to the user's most frequently visited Web sites or documents
History	Displays a list of Web pages that were recently visited
Mail	Opens Outlook Express for sending and receiving e-mail; enables the user to send a link or a page to someone, or to start reading newsgroups
Print	Prints the current Web page
Edit	Opens the current Web page in a Web page editor, such as Word

5 Move the mouse pointer to the Address bar.

The Address bar is where you enter the address or URL of the Web page you want to access. You will learn more about URLs in the next section.

6 Move the mouse pointer to the separator bar to the left of the Links toolbar.

The mouse pointer changes to a double-sided arrow.

7 With the mouse pointer looking like a double-sided arrow, click and drag the separator bar to the left to expose more of the Links toolbar.

8 Move the mouse pointer to the vertical scroll bar at the right of the screen. This bar allows you to move the Web page up or down.

9 Move the mouse pointer to the status bar at the bottom of the screen.

When a Web page is loading, the left side of the bar displays the loading progress. The right side will display a lock icon if you are on a secure site. A secure site has been set up to prevent unauthorized people from seeing the information that is sent to it or from it.

10 To close Internet Explorer 5, click the Close button ⊠ in the upper right corner of the screen.

11 Follow the correct procedures to disconnect from your Internet Service Provider. You should be back to your desktop.

Navigating the Web

To access a Web page you need to enter the *Uniform Resource Locator (URL)* in the Address bar. A URL is an Internet addressing procedure that defines the route to a file or program. Each file on the Web has its own URL that uniquely identifies it. Once the URL for a Web page is entered, Internet Explorer will locate that particular file and display it. Using the Explorer toolbar buttons, you can navigate around that Web site. If a button on the toolbar is dimmed, it is unavailable for use. For example, you have to click a link to jump to at least one other page before the Back button becomes available. Once you click a link, the letters on the Back button turn black, meaning that action is available. Clicking the Back button takes you back to the page you just visited. Clicking the Home button takes you to the default home page for the computer you are using.

steps

1. Connect to your Internet Service Provider and then click the Explorer icon

2. Position the mouse pointer at the end of the URL in the Address bar and click the left mouse button.

   The mouse pointer turns into an I-beam and the entire address is selected.

3. Key the address **www.sony.com** and then press Enter.

   The home page for the Sony company is displayed as shown in Figure WIN3.3. Your screen will probably look different as Web pages are updated frequently.

   FIGURE WIN3.3 The Sony Home Page

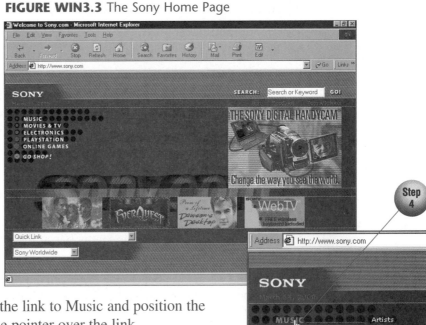

4. Find the link to Music and position the mouse pointer over the link.

   The mouse pointer turns into a hand with a pointing index finger. This is the icon the mouse pointer changes to whenever it is over a link that will jump you to another Web page.

(5) Click the Music link.

(6) Find the link to Artists and click it.

(7) Click the Back button ⬅ to go back to the last page you visited.

(8) Click the Back button again to move back to the Sony home page.

(9) Click the Forward button ➡ to move forward to the Music page.

(10) Click the Forward button again to move forward to the Artists page.

(11) Click the Home button 🏠 to jump immediately to your home page.

The options of going Back, Forward, and Home are also available by clicking View and then Go To on the Menu bar.

(12) Click the down arrow ▼ to the right of the Address bar. In the list of addresses that display, click the address for the Sony Web site.

Internet Explorer remembers the last Web page addresses you entered. The address for the Sony Web site is at the top of the displayed drop-down list.

(13) Click View on the Menu bar, point to Go To, and then click Home Page.

(14) Close the browser and disconnect from the Internet.

Parts of the URL

In general, a URL is made up of three parts. For example, look at the following URL for the Library of Congress:

http://www.loc.gov/

The first part of a URL—*http://* in the example—identifies what *protocol* is being used. Whenever data is sent from one computer to another, certain rules, or protocols, must be followed for the transmission to be successful. Many protocols are used on the Internet. The Hypertext Transfer Protocol (http) is the protocol used to transfer World Wide Web pages from one computer to another.

The second part of the URL—*www.* in the example—is format information, such as www for Web pages. The next part of a URL is the *domain name,* or the name of the host computer site. This part of the URL usually ends with a period, or dot as it is called, followed by a domain suffix of three letters. These three letters are an abbreviation for the type of organization hosting the Web site. Following is a list of some of the more common abbreviations and what they stand for:

com	company or commercial organization
edu	educational institution
gov	government site
mil	military site
net	companies and groups involved with the administration of the Internet
org	organization, typically non-profit

If you were to enter *http://www.loc.gov* in the Address bar, you would be taken to the home page for the Library of Congress. This is a very large Web site with many pages branching off the home page, each of which is indicated by a forward slash following the domain suffix—for example, http://www.loc.gov/copyright.

Adding a Web Page
to the Favorites List

When you find a Web site that you especially like or a site you probably will visit frequently, you will want a quick way to return to it without having to navigate through a long succession of linked sites or keep track of its URL. The Favorites feature in Internet Explorer 5 allows you to save favorite sites to the Favorites menu. Once a Web site has been saved in the Favorites menu, you can return to it quickly by clicking its name on the menu.

steps

1 Connect to your Internet Service Provider and then click the Explorer icon .

2 Position the mouse pointer at the end of the URL in the Address bar and click the left mouse button.

The mouse pointer turns into an I-beam and the entire address is selected.

3 Key the address **www.animal.discovery.com** and then press Enter.

4 Click the Favorites button to display the Favorites pane to the left of the screen as shown in Figure WIN3.4.

FIGURE WIN3.4 The Favorites Panel

5 Click Favorites on the Menu bar and then click Add to Favorites.

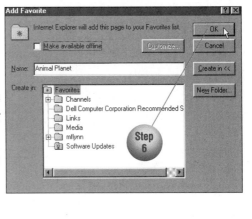

6 At the Add Favorite dialog box, click OK.

The Animal Planet Web site is added to the end of the Favorites menu.

7 Position the mouse pointer at the end of the URL in the Address bar and click the left mouse button.

The mouse pointer turns into an I-beam and the entire address is selected.

8 Key the address **www.sandiegozoo.org**. Press Enter.

9 Click Favorites on the Menu bar and then click Add to Favorites. Click OK.

The San Diego Zoo Web site is added to the end of the Favorites menu. In the future, you can jump directly to this site by first clicking Favorites and then the Web site name in the list.

10 Position the mouse pointer at the end of the URL in the Address bar and click the left mouse button.

The mouse pointer turns into an I-beam and the entire address is selected.

11 Key the address **www.iams.com**. Press Enter.

12 Click Favorites on the Menu bar and then click Add to Favorites. Click OK.

The Iams Company Web site is added to the end of the Favorites menu.

13 Click the Animal Planet link on the Favorites menu.

You jump to the Animal Planet Web site.

14 Click the Close button in the upper right corner of the Favorites pane.

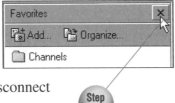

15 Close the browser and disconnect from the Internet.

Adding a Shortcut to the Desktop

Take 2

Another way to save your favorite sites is to create shortcuts on your desktop. After you create the shortcut, you jump to the site by double-clicking its icon on the desktop. To create a shortcut to a favorite Web site:

1 Display the Web page to which you want to create a shortcut.
2. Click File, point to Send, and then click Shortcut to Desktop

Organizing the Favorites List

Once you have added several Web sites to the Favorites list, it may become difficult to use because you must look through a long list to find the particular Web site you want. To solve this problem, you can organize the list by grouping similar sites together in a folder. New folders can be added to the list, sites can be moved into folders, the name of a folder or a Web site can be changed, and sites can be deleted from the list. The Organize Favorites option on the Favorites menu enables you to keep your Favorites list organized.

steps

1 Connect to your Internet Service Provider and then click the Explorer icon 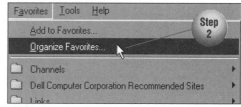.

2 Click Favorites on the Menu bar and then click Organize Favorites.

The Organize Favorites dialog box is displayed.

3 Click the Create Folder button.

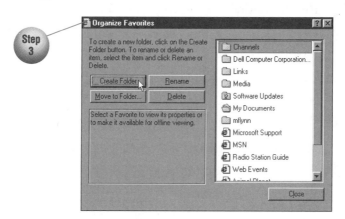

4 A new folder appears at the bottom of the list. Key **Animals**.

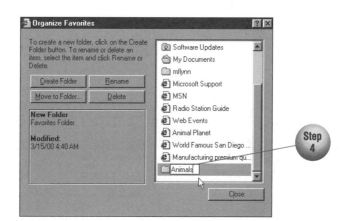

5 Click the link to *Animal Planet* and then click the Move to Folder button.

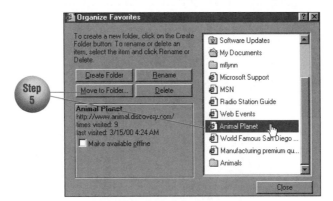

6 At the Browse for Folder dialog box, click the *Animals* folder and then click the OK button.

The link to the Animal Planet Web site is moved into the *Animals* folder.

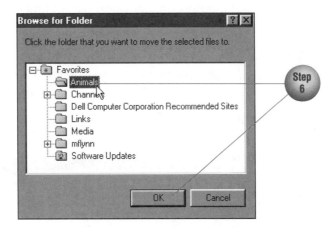

7 Click the link to the World Famous San Diego Zoo and then click the Move to Folder button.

8 At the Browse for Folder dialog box, click the *Animals* folder and then click the OK button.

The link to the San Diego Zoo Web site is moved into the *Animals* folder.

9 Click the link that says *Manufacturing premium*. This is the link to the Iams company. Then click the Move to Folder button.

10 At the Browse for Folder dialog box, click the *Animals* folder and then click the OK button.

The link to the Iams Web site is moved into the *Animals* folder.

11 Click the Close button.

(continued)

12 Click Favorites on the Menu bar. Point to the *Animals* folder submenu that displays at the bottom of the list. Click Animal Planet.

You jump to the Animal Planet Web site.

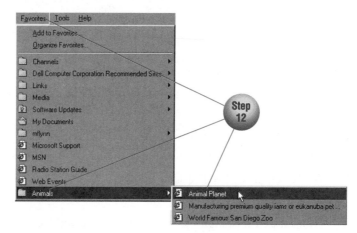

13 Click Favorites on the Menu bar and then click Organize Favorites.

The Organize Favorites dialog box is displayed.

14 You want to rename one of the Web sites. Click the *Animals* folder. In the list of Web sites that displays, click the option that says Manufacturing premium and then click the Rename button.

The name of the Web site is highlighted.

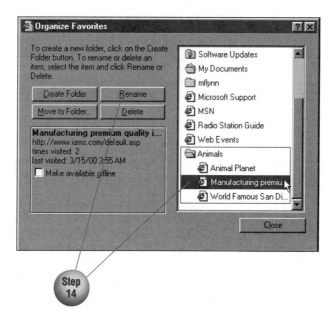

15 Key **Iams** and then press Enter.

16 Next you want to delete a Web site from the list. Click the link to the World Famous San Diego Zoo and then click the Delete button.

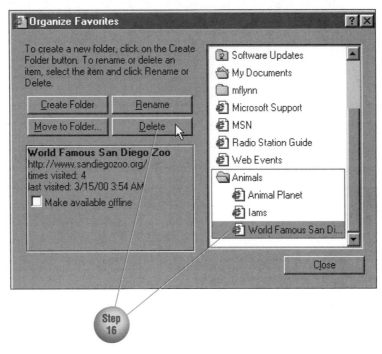

Step 16

17 At the Confirm File Delete dialog box, click <u>Y</u>es.

Problem ?

If you accidentally delete a site, you can restore it by double-clicking the Recycle Bin on the desktop. Select the site that was accidentally deleted. Click <u>F</u>ile on the Menu bar and then click <u>R</u>estore.

18 Click the C<u>l</u>ose button.

19 Close the browser and disconnect from the Internet.

Searching
the Web

The amount of information available on the World Wide Web is phenomenal. Data on any topic you might want to research is most likely available somewhere on the Web. The question is, with so much information out there, how can you begin to find what you are looking for? A special class of software called *search engines* are available to help you locate material on any topic on the Web. A search engine is a program that you access remotely in order to perform keyword searches. The search engine gathers data about topics available at Web sites and then stores this data in a database that is indexed by topic. You enter keywords that define what you are looking for. The search engine searches its database for your keywords and returns anything that matches. In this way you are led to Web pages that have information related to your search topic.

steps

1. Connect to your Internet Service Provider and then click the Explorer icon .

2. Click the Search button .

   The Search Explorer bar is displayed at the left side of the screen. Several categories for the search are available, such as find an address or find a business. Find a Web page is the default category.

3. Click in the Find a Web page containing text box and key **dogs**.

4. Click the Search button located beneath the text box.

   A list of links to suggested Web pages is displayed. (Your list may look different from the one shown here.) Several search engines are available with the Search feature in Internet Explorer. The list of links will vary depending on which search engine was used to conduct the search.

5. Scroll down the Search Explorer bar to see more suggested sites. The first 10 sites are listed.

6. At the bottom of the Search Explorer bar, click the more results> link to display the next 10 sites.

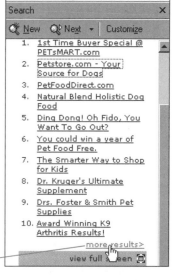

?

Problem

If you do not see a more results> link at the bottom of the Search Explorer bar, a different search engine was used to do the search. There will be a link to take you to the next 10 options. It may be called next> or next 10> or something similar.

7 Look at the next 10 links. Click the <previous results link to display the first 10 results.

8 If you see the link for Petstore.com, click it. If not, select another link to click.

9 The Web page is displayed. To see more of the Web page, click the Close button in the Search window.

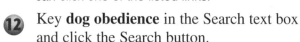

10 Click the Search button to display the Search Explorer bar.

11 Click the down arrow next to the Next button at the top of the Search Explorer bar. The drop-down menu that is displayed lists all the search engines available with the Search feature. Click InfoSeek.

The InfoSeek search engine is now available. You can either enter a new keyword in the Search textbox or you can click one of the listed links.

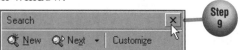

12 Key **dog obedience** in the Search text box and click the Search button.

13 Scroll down the window to the Search Results section. Click the first link, The Dog Obedience and Training Page.

14 Click the Close button ☒ at the top of the Search Explorer bar.

15 Browse the information provided at this site.

16 Close the browser and disconnect from the Internet.

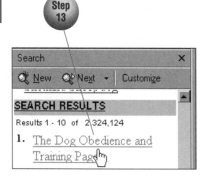

Conducting Advanced Searches

The links to sites that are listed as the result of a search using a search engine are called *hits*. Often a search will result in hundreds of thousands of hits—obviously too many for you to review. Search engines list the hits that are most relevant at the top of the list, which is helpful. But conducting a search that eliminates as many irrelevant hits as possible is more efficient. One technique is to refine your keywords so they are as specific as possible. If you are searching for a specific phrase, place the phrase within quotation marks. For example, if you used the keywords *chocolate cake* in a search, the search engine would return all hits that included both *chocolate* and *cake*. The two words would not necessarily have to appear together. If, however you put quotation marks around the words as in "chocolate cake," the hit would have to have the keywords exactly as they appear between the quotation marks. You can also use the Boolean operators AND, OR, and NOT to create relationships among the keywords in your search query. If keywords are joined with the operator AND, both words must be present, as in cats AND dogs. If keywords are joined with the operator OR, either one or the other word must be present, as in puppies OR dogs. If keywords are joined with the operator NOT, the first word must be present and the second word cannot be present. Many search engines allow you to use the plus sign, +, in place of AND and the minus sign, –, in place of NOT. You can also use wildcards to help refine the search. The asterisk, for example, typically replaces multiple characters. Using the keyword *fish**, for example, would find *fishing*, *fishes*, *fished*, *fishery*, and so on.

steps

1. Connect to your Internet Service Provider and then click the Explorer icon .

2. Position the mouse pointer at the end of the URL in the Address bar and click the left mouse button.

   The mouse pointer turns into an I-beam and the entire address is selected.

3. Key the address **www.northernlight.com**. Press Enter.

   The home page for Northern Light is displayed.

4. Key **canoe outfitter** in the Search for text box. Press the Search button.

   More than 16,000 matches were found. All hits that are indexed with the word *canoe* and the word *outfitter* are found. The search engine is not looking for the exact phrase *canoe outfitter*. In order for the search engine to find the exact phrase, you must place it within quotation marks.

5. In the Find this text box, place quotation marks around the phrase *canoe outfitter*. Click the Search button.

   The results are narrowed down to around 11,000. You can narrow the results further by adding a more specific keyword.

(6) In the Find this text box, key **AND "boundary waters"** after the phrase *"canoe outfitter."* Click the Search button.

Now there are a little over 2,000 hits.

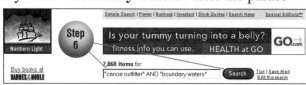

(7) In the Find this text box, key **NOT Canada** after the phrase "boundary waters." Click the Search button.

The results are narrowed down to about 375 hits. Using *Canada* as a keyword means that words such as *Canadian* are not included.

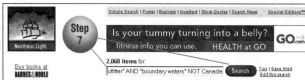

To make sure the keyword includes anything related to Canada, you must use a wildcard.

(8) Delete the word *Canada* and key **Canad*** in its place.

The results are narrowed down to about 266 hits.

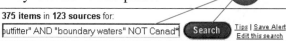

(9) Find the link *A Boundary Waters Canoe Outfitter Voyageur* and click it.

(10) When the site's home page is displayed, click the Print button on the toolbar.

(11) Close your browser and disconnect from the Internet.

Choosing a Search Service

Take 2

Two types of search services are available on the Web: subject directories and search engines. Each one of these search services has its advantages and disadvantages. A subject directory groups Web sites by topic, such as art, entertainment, or health. Employees of the search service company do all the indexing. Each site must meet a certain standard of quality before it is included in the index. Checking the quality of each Web site is time-consuming; therefore, subject directories can only index a fraction of the Web sites available. An advantage of a subject directory is that most of the pages indexed in it are valuable. A disadvantage is that fewer sites are indexed. Yahoo (www.yahoo.com) is an example of a subject directory.

Instead of being indexed by humans, search engines are indexed by automated programs called *robots* or *spiders*. These programs roam the Web searching for new documents. When a new document is found, the program reports the document's address, retrieves part of the document's text, and adds the words to a huge database. An advantage of a search engine is that it is much more comprehensive than a subject directory. However, since no humans monitor the quality of the Web sites or their relevance, many of the indexed sites may be useless. Alta Vista (www.altavista.com) and InfoSeek (www.infoseek.com) are examples of search engines.

In general, start your searches using a subject directory since the quality of the Web sites is usually quite good. Then if you cannot find what you are looking for using a subject directory, use a search engine since many more Web sites will be indexed.

Reviewing
Web Channels

One way to get information from the Web is to access the Internet and retrieve the data. A second way to get information from the Web is to have it delivered to you via a channel. A channel is a Web site that is automatically updated on a regular basis. Channels use what is called "push," or broadcasting, technology to deliver information directly to customers. If you subscribe to a channel, you can have automatically updated content delivered to you and displayed in Internet Explorer or on your desktop. Say, for example, you are a dedicated sports fan. With a channel, you can have sports scores displayed on your desktop that are automatically updated throughout the day. You do not have to go out and find the information—it comes directly to you. In many ways, opening up a channel is like turning on a television channel. Internet Explorer provides some links to channels in the Channels folder located in the Favorites menu.

steps

1. Connect to your Internet Service Provider and then click the Explorer icon [icon].

2. Position the mouse pointer at the end of the URL in the Address bar and click the left mouse button.

   The mouse pointer turns into an I-beam and the entire address is selected.

3. Key the address **www.microsoft.com/windows/ie/ie40/gallery** and press Enter.

   The Web page for Microsoft Windows Technologies Active Desktop Gallery is displayed.

4. Click the link to sports and then click ESPN SportsZone.

5. Click Add to Active Desktop.

6. The Internet Explorer window is displayed asking if you want to add an Active Desktop item to your desktop. Click <u>Y</u>es.

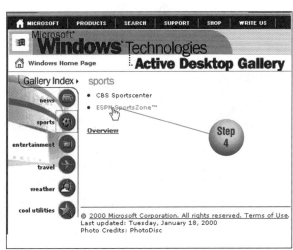

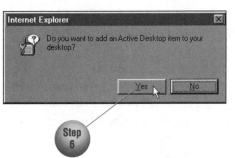

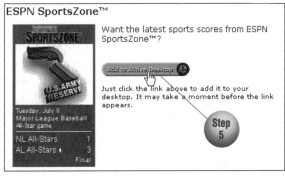

7 Another Internet Explorer window may appear asking if you want to enable your Active Desktop so that you can view items on your desktop. If it does, click <u>Y</u>es. If it does not, move on to Step 8.

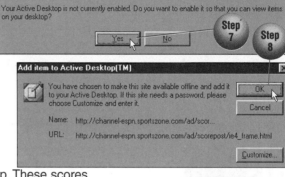

8 The Add item to Active Desktop window is displayed. Click OK.

A synchronizing dialog box will be displayed briefly.

9 Minimize any open windows.

You should see a box flashing the latest sports scores on your desktop. These scores will be automatically updated throughout the day.

Problem **?**

If you don't see the sports scores, try right-clicking the desktop. Point to <u>A</u>ctive Desktop on the shortcut menu. Make sure the View as <u>W</u>eb Page option has a check mark next to it.

10 To delete the channel from the Active Desktop, move the mouse pointer over the box displaying the scores. Click the down-arrow button in the upper left corner.

11 Click Customize my <u>D</u>esktop.

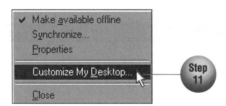

12 At the Display Properties dialog box, make sure the option for http://channel-espn.sportszone.com is selected. (There should be a checkmark next to it.) Click the <u>D</u>elete button.

13 At the Active Desktop Item dialog box asking if you are sure you want to delete the item from your desktop, click <u>Y</u>es.

14 Click the OK button in the display Properties dialog box.

The box with the sports scores should no longer be on the desktop.

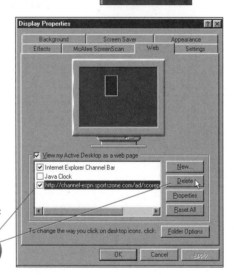

15 Make sure your usual desktop icons are displayed on the desktop. If they are not, right-click the desktop, point to <u>A</u>ctive Desktop on the shortcut menu, and click the View as <u>W</u>eb Page option.

16 Close the browser and disconnect from the Internet.

Copying Text from a Web Page

After you find information on the Web that you want to keep, what do you do with it? In an earlier exercise you learned you could print the Web page that is currently displayed by clicking the Print button on the Explorer toolbar. Just printing the current Web page is inefficient, however. Often what you want to keep is just the text on the Web page. But if you print the page, you end up printing several extraneous graphics that may be of little or no reference value. To avoid printing unwanted graphics, you can copy text to the clipboard and then paste it into a word processing program such as Microsoft WordPad.

steps

1 Connect to your Internet Service Provider and then click the Explorer icon.

2 Position the mouse pointer at the end of the URL in the Address bar and click the left mouse button.

The mouse pointer turns into an I-beam and the entire address is selected.

3 Key the address **www.britannica.com/bcom/dictionary/** and press Enter.

The Web page for Merriam-Webster's Collegiate Dictionary is displayed.

4 In the textbox, key **operating system** and then click the Find button.

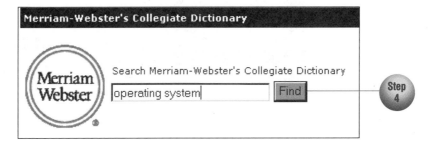

5 Place the mouse pointer at the beginning of the definition, to the left of the words *Main Entry*. When the mouse pointer turns into an I-beam, click and drag to the end of the definition.

The entire definition should be highlighted.

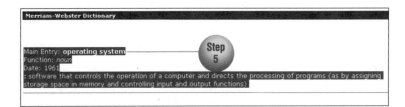

(6) On the Menu bar, click <u>E</u>dit and then click <u>C</u>opy.

The definition is now copied to the clipboard. The next step is to paste it into WordPad.

(7) Click the Start button on the Taskbar, point to <u>P</u>rograms, point to Accessories, and then click WordPad.

(8) Click the Paste button on the WordPad toolbar.

The text you copied is displayed in WordPad.

(9) Click the Print button on the WordPad toolbar.

(10) Click the Close button ⊠. Do not save the WordPad document.

(11) Close the browser and disconnect from the Internet.

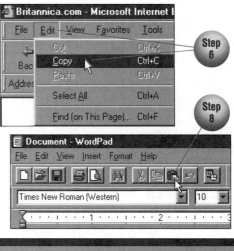

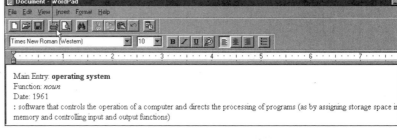

Main Entry: **operating system**
Function: *noun*
Date: 1961
: software that controls the operation of a computer and directs the processing of programs (as by assigning storage space in memory and controlling input and output functions)

Saving a Web Page

In addition to copying text from a Web page to the clipboard, you can save text from a Web page. Any document that Internet Explorer can display can be saved in four ways:

1) Web Page Complete, which saves all the files needed to display the page. Only the current Web page is saved. None of the linking pages are saved.
2) Web Archive, which saves a snapshot of the current Web page. With the Web Page Complete and Web Archive options, all of the Web page can be viewed offline.
3) Web Page HTML, which saves only the information on the Web page, not the graphics, sounds, or other files.
4) Text Only, which saves the information on the Web page in straight text format.

To save a Web page on your computer, click File on the Menu bar and then click Save As. At the Save As dialog box, double-click the folder in which the page is to be saved and enter a name for the page in the File name box. Click the down

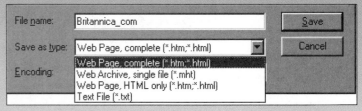

arrow to the right of the Save as type box. Select the file type you want from the options in the drop-down menu. The only file type that can be opened in either NotePad or WordPad is the Text Only option. The others must be opened in a word processing program capable of handling graphics, such as Microsoft Word.

Copying and Saving Graphics and Sound from a Web Page

Graphics on a Web page can be copied or saved. Copying a graphic places it on the clipboard. Once on the clipboard, the graphic can be pasted into a document in another application. Saving a graphic enables you to open it at a later time with a graphics program, or you can send it to someone as an e-mail attachment. Graphics are copied or saved by right-clicking on them.

steps

1 Connect to your Internet Service Provider and then click the Explorer icon .

2 Position the mouse pointer at the end of the URL in the Address bar and click the left mouse button. Then key the address **http://gallery.yahoo.com** and press Enter.

The Web page for the Yahoo! Picture Gallery is displayed.

3 Click on the featured picture.

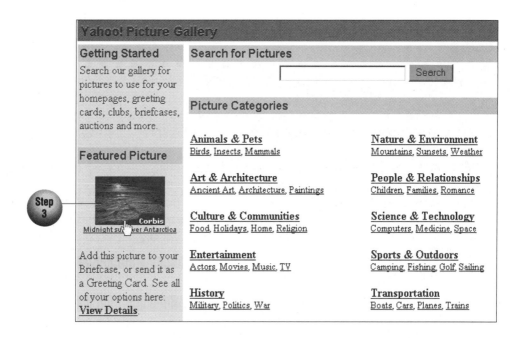

4 At the enlarged version of the picture that displays, right-click the picture and click the Save Picture As option.

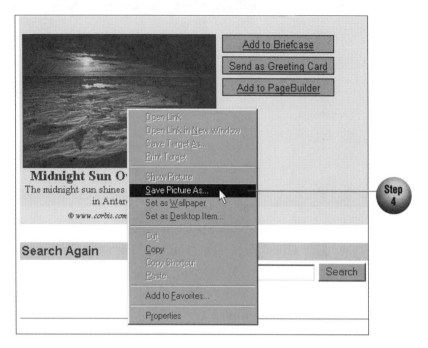

Step 4

5 At the Save Picture dialog box, click the down arrow to the right of the Save in box and then click Desktop.

6 Select the text currently in the File name box and key **graphic**. Then click the Save button.

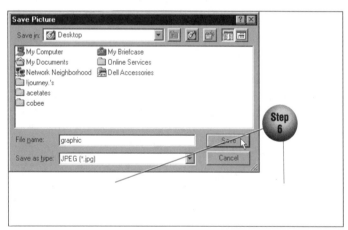

Step 6

7 Click the Start button on the Taskbar, point to Programs, point to Accessories, and then click Paint.

8 Click File on the Menu bar and then click Open.

9 At the Open dialog box that displays, click the down arrow to the right of the Look in box and click Desktop.

10 Click the down arrow to the right of the Files of type box and click the JPEG option.

(continued)

11 Click the graphic.jpg file and then click the Open button.

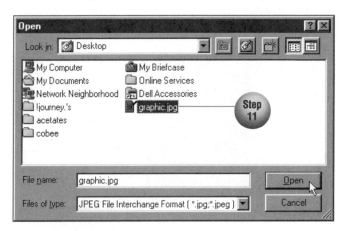

12 Click File, then Print, and then the OK button.

13 Click the Close button ⊠ to close the Paint program and return to Internet Explorer.

14 Position the mouse pointer at the end of the URL in the Address bar, click the left mouse button, and key the address **www.amazon.com**. Then press Enter.

The Web page for Amazon.com is displayed.

15 In the Search box, key **The Red Violin** and press the Go button.

16 Scroll down until you find the link for The Red Violin: Original Motion Picture Soundtrack. Click that link.

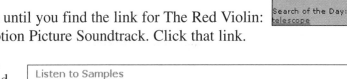

17 Scroll down until you find the Listen to Samples section. Click the link to Anna's Theme.

The Real Player dialog box is displayed.

Listen to Samples

To hear a song sample, click on the song titles below that are followed by ♪. Visit our audio help page for more information.

1. Anna's Theme ♪   **Step 17**
2. I. Cremona: Main Title ♪
3. I. Cremona: Death Of Anna ♪
4. I. Cremona: Birth Of The Red Violin ♪
5. I. Cremona: The Red Violin ♪
6. II. Vienna: The Monastery
7. II. Vienna: Kaspar's Audition/Journey To Vienna
8. II. Vienna: Etudes/Death Of Kaspar
9. III. Oxford: The Gypsies/Journey Across Europe
10. III. Oxford: Pope's Gypsy Cadenza

11. III. Oxford: Coitus Musicalis/Victoria's Departure
12. III. Oxford: Pope's Concert
13. III. Oxford: Pope's Betrayal
14. IV. Shanghai: Journey To China
15. IV. Shanghai: People's Revolution/Death Of Chou Yuan
16. V. Montreal: Morritz Discovers The Red Violin
17. V. Montreal: Morritz's Theme
18. V. Montreal: The Theft
19. V. Montreal: End Titles
20. 'The Red Violin': Chaconne For Violin And Orchestra

Problem?

In order to play the sample, RealPlayer must be installed on your computer. If it is not, click the Visit our audio help page link for more information and to download RealPlayer.

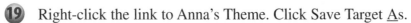

(18) After a few moments the sample is played. Click the close button ⊠ to close the Real Player dialog box.

(19) Right-click the link to Anna's Theme. Click Save Target As.

(20) At the Save As dialog box, click the down arrow to the right of the Save in box and then click Desktop.

(21) Select the text currently in the File name box and key **AnnasTheme**. Then click the Save button.

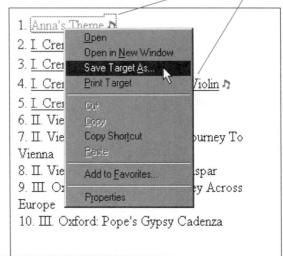

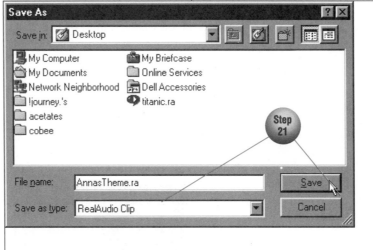

(22) Minimize any open window. When the desktop is displayed, double-click the icon for *AnnasTheme* ▭ .

The Real Player dialog box is displayed.

(23) After a few moments the sample is played. Click the close button ⊠ to close the Real Player dialog box.

(24) Close the browser and disconnect from the Internet.

(25) Drag the icons for *AnnasTheme* and *graphic.jpg* to the Recycle Bin.

(26) At the prompt asking if you really want to delete, click Yes.

Working with Hypermedia

By now you are familiar with hypertext on the Web. Hypertext links take you to other documents on the Web. Hypermedia is an extension of hypertext. Hypermedia integrates text, images, sound, graphics, animation, and video on the Web through hyperlinks. In order to utilize hypermedia, your computer must have a stereo sound card and stereo speakers. In addition, Microsoft Media Player must be installed.

steps

1 Connect to your Internet Service Provider and then click the Explorer icon [icon].

2 Position the mouse pointer at the end of the URL in the Address bar and click the left mouse button. Then key the address **www.cnn.com** and press Enter.

The Web page for the CNN is displayed.

3 Find the section called Video on Demand and click the Play Video link.

After a few moments the video will start playing.

Step 3

Problem

? If the video does not start playing, you may need to set the player and speed. Click the down arrow to the right of each box and select Real for the player and select your modem's speed for the speed.

4 When the video stops playing, click the Close button in the Real Player window.

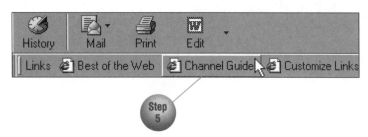

(5) Click the Channel Guide button on the Links toolbar.

Step
5

If the Channel Guide button does not display, move the mouse button to the separator bar to the left of the Links toolbar and then click and drag to the left until the button is displayed.

(6) At the WindowsMedia Web page that displays, click the Radio tab. Then click the Launch the Radio Tuner link.

The options for radio stations are displayed.

(7) The WindowsMedia.com Radio Tuner window is displayed. Double-click the link to VH1 atWork Radio.

It may take a minute or two, but eventually you will be connected to VH1 atWork Radio and the music will start playing.

Web pages change frequently. If these directions do not seem to match what you see on the screen, browse until you find a link to a radio station.

(8) Close the VH1 atWork Radio window. Then close the WindowsMedia.com Radio Tuner window.

(9) Close the browser and disconnect from the Internet.

Features Summary

Feature	Button	Menu	Keyboard
Add a Web page to Favorites list		Favorites, Add to Favorites	
Close Internet Explorer 5	✕	File, Close	
Copy text		Edit, Copy	Ctrl + C
Display list of recently visited Web pages	History	View, Explorer Bar, History	Ctrl + H
Launch Internet Explorer 5			
Move to previous page Insert	Back	View, Go To, Back	Alt + left arrow
Move to next page in a series of pages previously visited	Forward	View, Go To, Forward	Alt + right arrow
Move to user's home page	Home	View, Go To, Home Page	Alt + Home
Open the Search bar	Search	View, Explorer Bar, Search	Ctrl + E
Open the Favorites bar	Favorites	View, Explorer Bar, Favorites	Ctrl + I
Open Outlook Express for sending and receiving e-mail	Mail	Tools, Mail & News	
Open current Web page in a Web page editor	Edit	File, Edit	
Organize the Favorites list		Favorites, Organize Favorites	
Print the current Web page	Print	File, Print	Ctrl + P
Stop downloading a page	Refresh	View, Stop	Esc
Update the current page	Stop	View, Refresh	F5

Procedures Check

Matching: On the line provided, write the letter of the word that best matches the definition.

a. Back
b. Favorites
c. History
d. Home page
e. Hyperlink
f. Internet Service Provider
g. Intranet
h. Network

i. Print
j. Refresh
k. Search
l. Stop
m. URL
n. Web browser
o. World Wide Web

1. This term refers to a group of computers and other hardware devices that are joined together so that applications, data, and messages can be shared._____

2. This term refers to a collection of documents found all over the Internet that can be navigated using hyperlinks._____

3. If you click this spot in a document, you jump to another document. _____

4. This is the piece of software you need in order to navigate the World Wide Web. _____

5. This term refers to a private collection of networks found within a corporation. _____

6. This term refers to a company that offers Internet access to subscribers for a small monthly fee._____

7. This term refers to the top-level page of any Web site. _____

8. Click this button to return to a previously visited Web page. _____

9. Click this button to update the current Web Page. _____

10. Click this button to make a hard copy of a Web page. _____

11. Click this button to open a bar that enables you to search the Web._____

12. Click this button to display a list of Web pages that were recently visited._____

13. Opens a bar where you can store links to your most frequently visited Web sites.

14. Click this button to stop the downloading of a page. _____

15. This term refers to an addressing procedure used by the Internet that defines the route to a file or program. _____

Skills Review

Activity 1: Navigating the Web and Adding Web Pages to the Favorites List

1 Connect to the Internet and access Internet Explorer.
2 In the Address bar, key the URL **www.weather.com**.
3 Under Local Weather there is a text box for entering a ZIP Code. Enter your ZIP Code and click Go. Look over the weather forecast for your city or town.
4 Click the Favorites button and add this Web page to your list of favorite Web sites.
5 Click the Back button.
6 In the text box under Local Weather, key the ZIP Code **96813** and click Go. Look over the weather forecast for Honolulu.
7 Click the Home button to return to your home page.
8 Disconnect from the Internet.

Activity 2: Adding a Folder to the Favorites List

1 Connect to the Internet and access Internet Explorer.
2 Click Favorites on the Menu bar and then click Organize Favorites. Click the Create Folder button. Create a folder named Movies.
3 In the Address bar, key the URL **www.imdb.com**.
4 To add this Web page to your *Movies* folder, click Favorites on the Menu bar and then click Add to Favorites. Click the *Movies* folder to open it. Click the OK button.
5 In the Search text box, enter the name of your favorite movie and click the Go button. Read some of the information about your favorite movie.
6 In the Address bar, key the URL **http://www.mrshowbiz.go.com**.
7 Repeat step 4 to add this page to the *Movies* folder.
8 Search the Web site to find a review of a movie that you would like to go see.
9 Disconnect from the Internet.

Activity 3: Searching the Web

1 Connect to the Internet and access Internet Explorer.
2 Click the Search button and search for Oscar Awards.
3 Find a Web site related to the Oscar Awards that interests you and go to that Web site.
4 Add the Web site to your *Movies* folder on the Favorites list.
5 Click the down arrow to the right of the Next button and choose a different search engine.
6 Enter the name of your favorite actor or actress.
7 Find a Web site from the list of sites that interest you and go to that Web site.
8 Add the Web site to your *Movies* folder on the Favorites list.
9 Disconnect from the Internet.

Activity 4: Conducting an Advanced Search

1 Connect to the Internet and access Internet Explorer.
2 Key **www.northernlight.com** in the Address bar.
3 Key **"independent films"** in the Search text box and click the Search button. Notice how many matches were found.
4 Add **AND festivals** after *"independent films"* in the Search text box and click the Search button. Notice how many matches were found.
5 Add **NOT Europe** after *AND festivals* in the Search text box and click the Search button. Notice how many matches were found.
6 Find a Web site from this list that interests you and go to that Web site.
7 Add the Web site to your *Movies* folder on the Favorites list.
8 Disconnect from the Internet.

Activity 5: Copying Graphics

1 Connect to the Internet and access Internet Explorer.
2 Click Favorites on the Menu bar, point to the *Movies* folder, and click The Internet Movie Database option.
3 Click the link to Photo Galleries.
4 Find a link to one of your favorite movies and click it.
5 Click on a photo from the movie you selected to enlarge it.
6 Right-click the picture and click the Save Picture As option.
7 At the Save Picture dialog box that displays, click the down arrow to the right of the Save in box. Click Desktop. Select the text currently in the File name box and key an appropriate name. Click the Save button.
8 Click the Start button on the Taskbar, point to Programs, point to Accessories, and then click Paint.
9 Click File on the Menu bar and then click Open.

10 At the Open dialog box that displays, click the down arrow to the right of the Look in box and click Desktop. Click the down arrow to the right of the Files of type box and click the JPEG option. Click the name of the graphic file you just saved and then click the Open button.

11 Click File and then click Print. Click the OK button.

12 Close the Paint program.

13 Drag the icon for the photo from the desktop to the Recycle Bin.

14 Disconnect from the Internet.

Activity 6: Accessing Hypermedia

1 Connect to the Internet and access Internet Explorer.

2 Key **www.centerseat.com** in the Address bar.

3 A window is displayed from which you can select the connection speed of your modem. Click the appropriate option for your modem.

4 Click the Screen link.

5 Click the Tracking Trailers link.

6 Watch the current trailer.

7 Disconnect from the Internet.

Performance Plus

Activity 1: Adding a Folder to the Favorites List, Adding Web Sites to a Folder, and Organizing a Folder

1 Connect to the Internet and access Internet Explorer.

2 Create a Folder named Pizza in the Favorites List.

3 Key **www.pizzahut.com** in the Address bar.

4 Add this page to the *Pizza* folder in the Favorites list.

5 Key **www.dominos.com** in the Address bar.

6 Add this page to the *Pizza* folder in the Favorites list.

7 Use the search feature to find the Domino's that delivers to you.

8 Key **www.papajohns.com** in the Address bar.

9 Add this page to the *Pizza* folder in the Favorites list.

10 Use the Organize Favorites option in the Favorites menu to rename the link to the Domino's home page to **Domino's**.

11 Use the Organize Favorites option in the Favorites menu to delete the Web page for Papa John's Pizza.

12 Disconnect from the Internet.

Activity 2: Using Hypermedia

1 Connect to the Internet and access Internet Explorer.
2 Key **www.topsecretrecipes.com/tvtime/tvtime.htm** in the Address bar.
3 Click the link for Streaming Video.
4 Click the link to your modem speed for one of the TV shows you would like to watch.
5 When the clip finishes playing, close the Windows Media window.
6 Click the link to Streaming Audio.
7 Click a link to an Audio clip you would like to hear.
8 When the clip finishes playing, close the RealPlayer window.
9 Disconnect from the Internet.

Activity 3: Searching the World Wide Web, Copying Text from a Web Page, and Saving a Graphic Image

1 Connect to the Internet and access Internet Explorer.
2 Use a search engine to find Web sites related to the history of pizza.
3 Find a Web site that explains the history of pizza and when the first pizzeria opened in the United States. Use several different search engines.
4 Add the Web site to the *Pizza* folder in the Favorites list.
5 Use a search engine to find a good recipe for pizza.
6 Copy the recipe and paste it into WordPad.
7 Print the recipe.
8 Close WordPad. Do not save the recipe.
9 Use a search engine to find some free clipart of pizza. When you find an image you like, save it to the desktop.
10 Open the graphic image of the pizza in Paint and print it.
11 Close Paint.
12 Disconnect from the Internet.

Activity 4: Finding Information on Internet Explorer's Automatic Search Feature

1 Connect to the Internet and access Internet Explorer.
2 Use Internet Explorer's Help feature to learn how to perform an automatic search from the Address bar and print the information.
3 Search for Pizzeria Uno using an automatic search from the Address bar.
4 Add the Web site to the *Pizza* folder on the Favorites list.
5 Search for pizza recipes using an automatic search from the Address bar.
6 Open WordPad. Write an explanation of the difference between using the Search button and using an automatic search from the Address bar. Explain which method you think is better for conducting searches and why.
7 Print your document, but do not save it.
8 Close WordPad.
9 Disconnect from the Internet.

Windows 98
Managing E-Mail with Outlook Express

Electronic mail, or e-mail, is probably the most popular service provided by the Internet. With e-mail you can send a message from one computer to another over the World Wide Web network. You compose an e-mail message using an e-mail software program. Windows 98 includes an e-mail program called Outlook Express. As in mail sent through the U.S. Postal Service, an e-mail message has to be addressed to the recipient. An e-mail address is the address of that individual's electronic mailbox. Just as a person's mailing address denotes a specific mailbox on a specific street, an e-mail address denotes a specific electronic mailbox on a specific computer. Your e-mail is stored in your electronic mailbox until you retrieve it. E-mail messages can be read, saved, deleted, printed, or sent on to someone else.

The Postal Service can take weeks to deliver a letter, depending on its destination. E-mail, on the other hand, is typically delivered in a matter of minutes—even if it is being sent to someone living on the other side of the world. Because of the incredible speed at which e-mail is delivered, compared to the delivery speed of the Postal Service, e-mail fans often refer to the U.S. Postal Service as "snail mail." Other than the monthly fee you pay to your Internet Service Provider, there is no charge for sending e-mail regardless of how far the message has to travel or how long it is.

Another feature provided by the Internet is an electronic discussion group service called Usenet. Usenet is a network of computers through which users exchange articles on topics of mutual interest. Each discussion group, or newsgroup, focuses on one subject. One can find a Usenet newsgroup on every topic imaginable, from cows to geomechanics. People post messages related to the newsgroup's topic. Anyone can read these messages and post replies, which are thus available for other group members to read. Some newsgroups contain worthwhile and useful information. Others contain nothing of value and are a waste of time.

Exercise caution when accessing newsgroups. Remember that anyone can post a message to a newsgroup. Quite often, the people posting messages are knowledgeable about the particular subject and have valuable information to share. But they also could be con artists trying to promote their own interests. Certain newsgroups are moderated, which means someone reads every single message to make sure it is relevant to that newsgroup. Other newsgroups are not moderated and their content may be questionable and controversial. Despite the need for caution, however, you are likely to find several newsgroups offering information of particular value to you. In this section, you will learn the following skills:

Skills

- Start and close Outlook Express
- Add a signature to messages
- Create and send e-mail
- Read and respond to e-mail
- Print and delete messages
- Attach a file to a message
- Open a file attached to a message
- Subscribe to and unsubscribe from mailing lists
- Subscribe to newsgroups
- Read newsgroup messages and post new messages
- Reply to an existing newsgroup message

Starting and Closing Outlook Express

Before you can send or receive e-mail messages you must connect to your Internet Service Provider. Once you have connected to the Internet you are ready to start Outlook Express. An option for Outlook Express is included on the Start menu. In addition, a shortcut to Outlook Express is offered on the Quick Launch toolbar that is on the Taskbar to the right of the Start button. A shortcut icon for Outlook Express may also be on the desktop. Once Outlook Express is started, you can check your e-mail and read your messages, reply to messages you have received, send new messages, or delete messages. To close Outlook Express you can either choose File and then click Exit, or you can click the Close button in the upper right corner of the window.

steps

1 Connect to your Internet Service Provider. Then click the Outlook Express button on the Taskbar.

Step 1

Once Outlook Express starts, you will see the Folders list to the left of the screen. Under the top folder, which is *Outlook Express*, are several subfolders. If the *Outlook Express* folder is selected, a Start page is displayed on the right. Under *Outlook Express* is an *Inbox* subfolder. The default setting is for Outlook Express to place any incoming mail in the *Inbox* folder. The number in brackets to the right of the *Inbox* folder indicates how many unread messages the folder contains.

2 Click the *Inbox* folder.

Your screen should look similar to Figure WIN4.1. At the top of the screen is the Menu bar and under the Menu bar is the Outlook Express toolbar. The functions of the buttons on the Outlook Express toolbar are explained in Table WIN4.1.

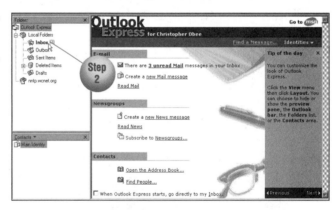

Step 2

FIGURE WIN4.1 Outlook Express Window

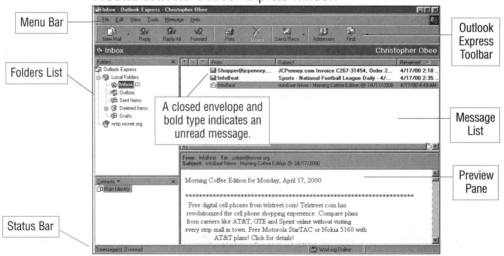

Menu Bar

Folders List

A closed envelope and bold type indicates an unread message.

Status Bar

Outlook Express Toolbar

Message List

Preview Pane

TABLE WIN4.1 Explorer Toolbar Buttons

Button	Function
New Mail	Displays a blank New Message window enabling the user to create a new e-mail message
Reply	Sends an e-mail message directly to the sender of the currently selected message
Reply All	Sends a reply to the author of the currently selected e-mail message as well as to everyone listed in the Cc: list
Forward	Forwards the selected e-mail message to one or more recipients
Print	Prints the currently selected message
Delete	Deletes the currently selected message
Send/Recv	Connects to the mail server automatically downloading any new mail and sending any outgoing messages
Addresses	Displays the address book where commonly used e-mail addresses can be stored
Find	Finds messages in the message folders based on search criteria the user enters

(3) Click the *Outbox* folder.

The default folders are *Inbox, Outbox, Sent Items, Deleted Items,* and *Drafts.*

(4) Click the *Sent Items* folder.

The *Sent Items* folder keeps copies of any e-mail you send.

(5) Click the *Deleted Items* folder.

The *Deleted Items* folder lists the e-mail messages you have received and deleted.

(6) Click the *Drafts* folder.

The *Drafts* folder stores a message you have started writing but have not sent. The message is unfinished, or you may have decided to rethink your message.

(7) Use your mouse to navigate the Outlook Express window, noting the location of the areas identified in Figure WIN4.1.

The Message list itemizes the messages contained in the folder currently selected in the Folders list. The Preview pane displays the message currently selected in the Message list. The Status bar displays the total number of messages in the folder currently selected in the Folders list. It also displays the number of those messages that have not yet been read. In the Message list, a closed envelope icon and bold type indicates an unread message.

(8) Click the Close button in the upper right corner of the Outlook Express window to close Outlook Express.

(9) Follow the correct procedures to disconnect from your Internet Service Provider.

Step 8

Inbox - Outlook Express - Christopher Obee

File   Edit   View   Tools   Message   Help

Adding a Signature
to Messages

The Signature feature of Outlook Express automatically adds information about the sender of the message to the end of every message he or she sends. Typically a signature includes information such as the user's name, title, e-mail address, Web page address, business telephone number, or favorite quotation. Sometimes people even create simple pictures using the characters on the keyboard. A signature should be no longer than four lines. Although it is appropriate to include your business phone number and address, do not include personal information such as your home address or home telephone number. Any personal information you need to provide to someone should be contained within the body of the e-mail message.

steps

1. Connect to your Internet Service Provider. Then click the Outlook Express button on the Taskbar.

2. Click Tools on the Menu bar and then click Options.

3. At the Options window, click the Signatures tab.

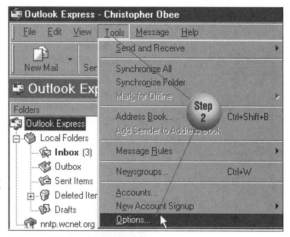

4. Click the New button. Then enter your name and your e-mail address in the Edit Signature box.

5. Select the Add signatures to all outgoing messages check box. Click OK.

   The signature will be added automatically to all of your messages. If this option is not selected, you can still add a signature to the messages you choose by clicking Insert on the Menu bar and then clicking Signature.

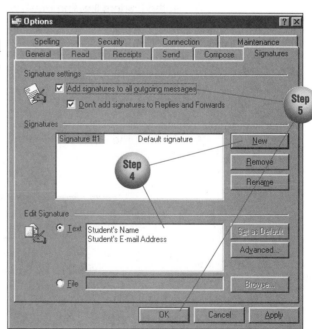

6 To see the signature, click the New Mail button.

The New Message window displays, and the signature you created is automatically entered in the message.

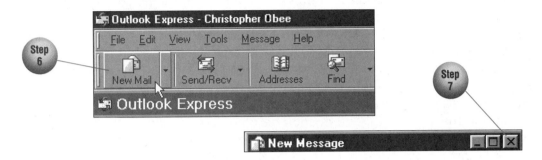

7 Click the Close button in the upper right corner of the New Message window.

8 Click the Close button ⊠ in the upper right corner of the Outlook Express window to close Outlook Express.

9 Follow the correct procedures to disconnect from your Internet Service Provider.

Creating and Sending E-Mail

You can quickly send an e-mail message to anyone with an e-mail address. All you need to do is enter the recipient's e-mail address, a subject line for the message, and the message itself. You can also send copies of the message to one or more people. E-mail addresses are made up of two parts that are separated by the @ symbol, which stands for the word "at." The user's name always comes before the @ symbol. This name is the account name for a particular user on the system. The user's location always comes after the @ symbol and provides the name of a system or location and a suffix identifying the type of organization (see Table WIN4.2 for a list of the common suffixes). The information in an e-mail address is separated by periods. As you move from left to right in the address, this information becomes less specific. At the far left is the user's name, followed by the name of a particular server, the name of an institution, and finally the type of institution. Most e-mail addresses conform to this pattern.

steps

1. Connect to your Internet Service Provider. Then click the Outlook Express button on the Taskbar.

2. Click the New Mail button [New Mail] .

   The New Message window is displayed.

3. In the To box, enter your e-mail address. Press tab to move to the Cc box.

4. With your instructor's approval, enter his or her e-mail address in the Cc box. Then press Tab to move to the Subject box.

   Cc traditionally has stood for "carbon copy," although with e-mail, the copies are electronic.

5. Key **Test** in the Subject box. Notice that the subject of the message appears in the Title bar of the window. Press Tab to move to the message area.

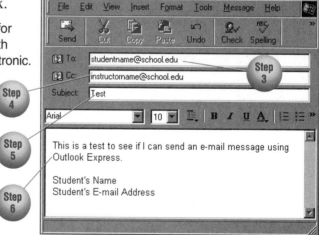

TABLE WIN4.2 Suffixes Used in E-Mail Addresses

Abbreviation	Organization
Com	Company or commercial organization
Edu	Educational institution
Gov	Government site
Mil	Military site
Net	Companies and groups involved with the administration of the Internet
Org	Organization

6 Key the following into the message area: **This is a test to see if I can send an e-mail message using Outlook Express.**

7 Click the Send button.

The message is sent electronically to your e-mail location, and a copy of the message is stored in the *Sent Items* folder.

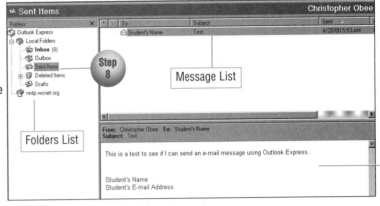

8 Click the *Sent Items* folder in the Folders list.

Three panes are now displayed. Notice that the name of the currently selected folder, *Sent Items*, appears in the bar at the top of the three panes. The Folders list is on the left, the Message list is at the upper right, and the Preview pane is at the lower right. Entries from the To and Subject boxes of the message you sent are displayed in the Message list. The body of the message is displayed in the Preview pane.

9 In the Folders list, click *Outlook Express*.

10 Click the Close button ✖ in the upper right corner of the Outlook Express window to close Outlook Express.

11 Follow the correct procedures to disconnect from your Internet Service Provider.

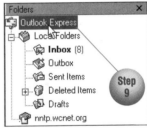

Formatting E-Mail Messages Using HTML Formatting

With Outlook Express you can create messages using HTML formatting, including graphics. Only mail programs that support HTML can read the formatting. If the recipient's mail program does not read HTML, the message is displayed as plain text with an HTML file attached. To set Outlook Express to use HTML formatting on all outgoing messages, go to the main window and click Tools, Options, and then the Send tab. In the Mail Sending Format section, click the HTML option. If you want to use HTML formatting on individual messages only, in an e-mail message window, click the Format menu. Make sure the Rich Text (HTML) option is selected (displays a black dot next to it).

HTML formatting makes it possible for you to use stationery for your e-mail messages. Stationery is a template that can include a background image, unique text font colors, and custom margins. To apply stationery to all of your outgoing messages, go to the main window and click Tools, Options, and then the Compose tab. Select the Mail option in the Stationery area and click the Select button. A window listing all of the stationery templates is displayed. Select an option and click OK. To apply stationery to individual messages, in an e-mail message window, click the Message menu, point to New Using, and then select a stationery template.

Take 2

Reading and Responding to E-Mail

When you connect to the Internet and start Outlook Express, any mail that has been sent to you is downloaded from your mail server to your computer. The number of new messages you have received appears in parentheses next to the Inbox in the Folders list. As long as you remain connected to the Internet, Outlook Express will automatically check for new messages at specified intervals. If you want to check for new messages immediately, you can click the Send/Recv button. When you receive a new message, you will hear a special sound that indicates you have new mail in your Inbox. To read a message, you must access the *Inbox* folder. Messages that have not been read are listed in bold in the Message list. You can see the first few lines of the selected message in the Preview pane. To open the message, double-click the message, and it will display in its own window.

steps

1. Connect to your Internet Service Provider. Then click the Outlook Express button on the Taskbar.

2. Click the *Inbox* folder.

   There should be at least one new message in your Inbox, which is indicated by the number in parentheses. This is the message you sent yourself in the previous exercise.

   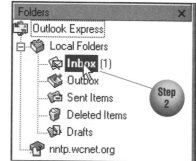

3. In the Message list, click the message you sent to yourself. You can now read the message in the Preview pane.

   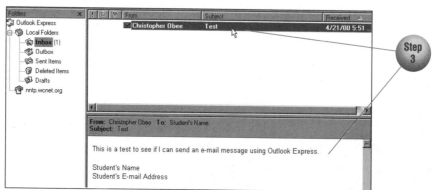

4. In the Message list, double-click the message you sent to yourself. The message opens in its own window.

5. In the message window, click the Reply button.

   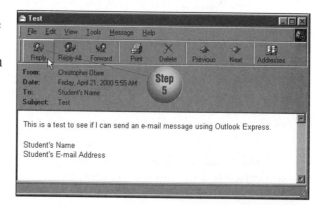

6. Key the following message: **Success! I have sent and received a message in Outlook Express.** Then click the Send button.

Notice that a copy of the original message is displayed at the bottom of the Reply window. The sender's e-mail address and subject are automatically entered.

7. Click the Close button ☒ in the upper right corner of the Outlook Express window to close Outlook Express.

8. Follow the correct procedures to disconnect from your Internet Service Provider.

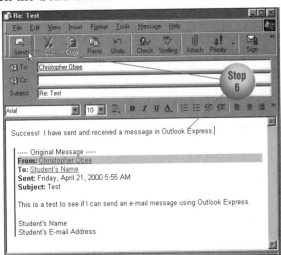

Sorting the Message List

The first screen below displays a Message list from Outlook Express. Notice that the envelope next to a message that you have not read is closed and the message appears in bold type. The envelope next to a message that has been read is open and the message is in regular type. At the top of the Message list are some buttons, three of which are From, Subject, and Received. By default, messages are sorted by the date they were received, with the most recently received messages at the bottom of the list. You also can sort the messages by the sender or by the entry in the subject line. For example, say you want all of the messages sent by the same person grouped together. Click the From button and Outlook Express will sort the Message list by Sender. The second screen below displays the Message list sorted by Sender.

From Button | Subject Button | Received Button

This message has been read.

This message has not been read.

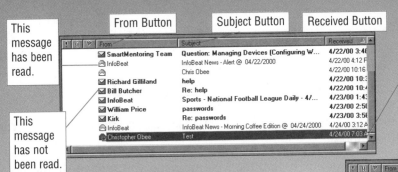

The default is for messages to be sorted by the date they were received with the most current messages being listed at the bottom of the list.

The messages in this Message list are sorted by Sender.

Clicking the Received button will sort the Message list by the date the message was received. Clicking the Received button once sorts the list from the message received the longest time ago to the most recently received message. Clicking the Received button a second time reverses the order. Clicking the button a third time changes the sort order back so the most recently received message is at the top of the list. The From and Subject buttons work the same way. Click them once and the list is sorted alphabetically from A to Z. Click them a second time and it is sorted from Z to A. Click them a third time and it is sorted from A to Z again.

Printing and Deleting Messages

There may be times when you want a hard copy of an e-mail message. Printing a message is simply a matter of pressing the Print button. Generally, once you have printed a message, you no longer need to keep the message in your *Inbox* folder and can delete it. For maintenance purposes, you should delete all e-mail messages that you no longer need. If you don't, your *Inbox* folder can quickly fill up with hundreds of messages. To delete a message, simply select the message and click the Delete button.

steps

1 Connect to your Internet Service Provider. Then click the Outlook Express button on the Taskbar.

2 If necessary, click the *Inbox* folder.

3 Find the first message you sent to yourself in the Message list (the subject is "Test"). Then double-click the message.

The message opens in its own window.

4 You want to print this message. Click the Print button.

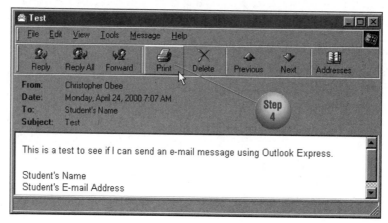

5 Once the message has printed, click the Close button ⊠ in the upper right corner of the window.

6 In the Message list, click (once) the first message you sent (it should be highlighted). Then click the Print button.

You do not have to open a message to print it. You can print a message by selecting it in the Message list and clicking the Print button.

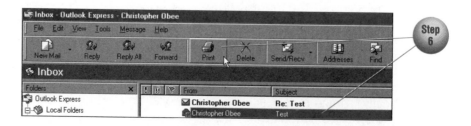

(7) Now you are ready to delete this message. With the message still highlighted in the Message list, click the Delete button.

The file is deleted from the Message list and moved to the *Deleted Items* folder.

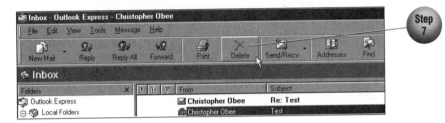

(8) Click the *Deleted Items* folder in the Folders list.

The message you just deleted is displayed in the Message list. Depending on how your system is set up, the files in the *Deleted Items* folder are removed from the computer when you exit the Outlook Express program, or they remain in the *Deleted Items* folder until you issue a command to remove them.

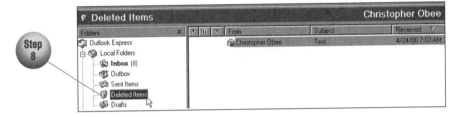

(9) You want to remove the file, or files, in the *Deleted Items* folder from the computer. Right-click the *Deleted Items* folder.

(10) At the shortcut menu that displays, click Empty 'Deleted Items' Folder.

(11) Click the Yes button when the warning box displays asking if you are sure you want to permanently delete the files.

There should be no messages in the Messages list.

(12) Click the Close button **[X]** in the upper right corner of the Outlook Express window to close Outlook Express.

(13) Follow the correct procedures to disconnect from your Internet Service Provider.

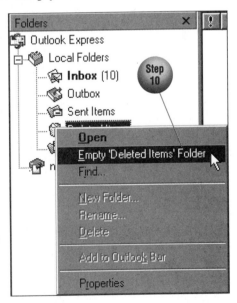

Attaching a File to a Message; Opening an Attachment

In certain situations, you may want to send someone an Excel or Word file you have created. Your instructor, for example, may ask you to submit an assignment by e-mail. You can do this by attaching the file to an e-mail message. Outlook Express sends the file to the recipient along with the e-mail message. Nearly any type of file can be attached to an e-mail message, including spreadsheets, documents, pictures, programs, sounds, and videos. The computer receiving the attached file must, however, have the necessary hardware and software to display or play the file. In the following exercise you will create a short document using WordPad and attach it to an e-mail message.

steps

1. From the Start menu, point to Programs, point to Accessories, and then click WordPad.

2. In the WordPad window, key the following: **I am going to attach this file to an Outlook Express e-mail message.**

3. Click File, then Save.

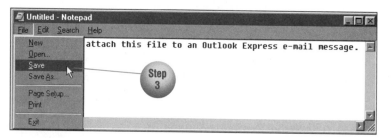

4. At the Save As window that displays, click the down arrow to the right of the Save in box. Then click Desktop.

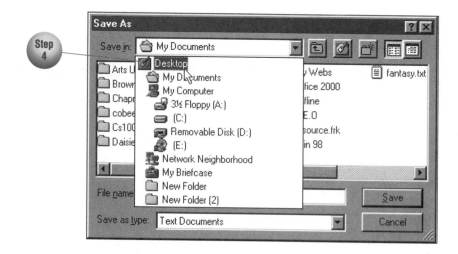

5 In the File name box, key **Attachment**. Then click Save.

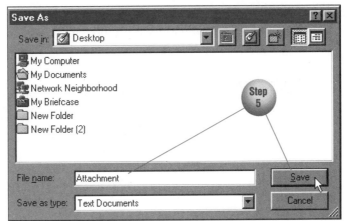

6 Click the Close button ☒ in the upper right corner of the WordPad window.

7 Connect to your Internet Service Provider. Then click the Outlook Express button on the Taskbar.

8 Click the *Inbox* folder, if necessary.

9 Click the New Mail button 🗋 .

10 Enter your e-mail address in the To box. With the approval of your instructor, enter his or her e-mail address in the Cc box. Key **Sending Attachment** in the Subject box. In the message area, key **This e-mail message has a file attached to it.**

11 Click the Attach button 📎 .

12 At the Insert Attachment window that displays, click the down arrow to the right of the Look in box. Then click Desktop.

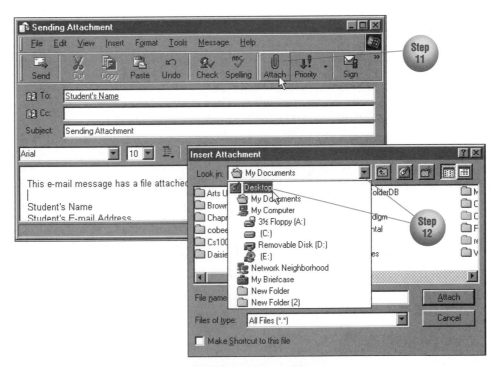

(continued)

13 Find the Attachmet.txt file and click it to select it. Then click the <u>A</u>ttach button.

Notice there is now an Attach box underneath the Subject box. In the Attach box is displayed the name of the file that is attached to the e-mail message.

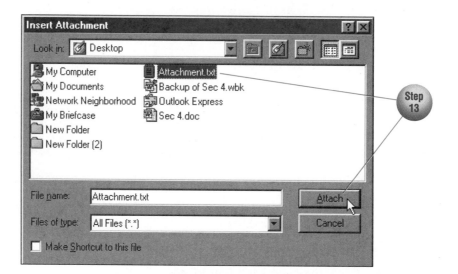

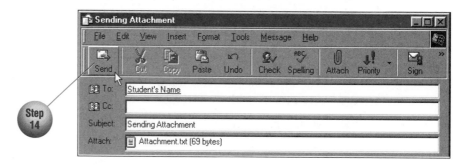

14 Click the Send button.

15 Click the Send/Recv button <img> to receive the message you just sent yourself.

To open a message that has a file attached to it, you must have the necessary hardware and software.

Problem

?

If you do not receive the message, wait a minute and click the Send/Recv button again. If after pressing the Send/Recv button a couple of times you still have not received the message, you may have to complete this exercise at another time.

16 The message you just sent should appear in the Message list with a paper clip icon next to it. Click the message to select it.

The message is displayed in the Preview pane.

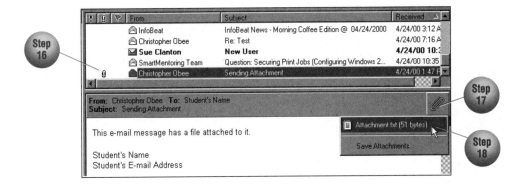

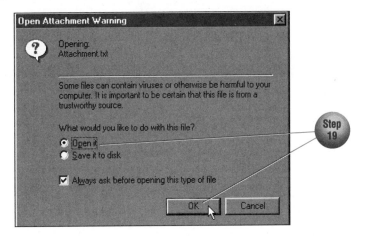

17. In the upper right corner of the Preview pane, click the Attachment button (includes a paper clip icon).

18. At the drop-down menu of file names, click *Attachment.txt* to open the file.

19. At the Open Attachment window that displays, click the Open it option and then click OK.

20. Close the file by clicking the Close button ☒ in the upper right corner of the window.

21. Click the Close button ☒ in the upper right corner of the Outlook Express window to close Outlook Express.

22. Follow the correct procedures to disconnect from your Internet Service Provider.

Subscribing to and
Unsubscribing from Mailing Lists

Many people enjoy participating in discussion groups on the Internet. Discussion groups bring together people with similar interests and provide a way for them to exchange ideas, share information, express their opinions, or socialize. Mailing lists are one form of discussion group. Another form is Usenet newsgroups, which is discussed later in this section.

Mailing lists are managed by Listserv software. Listserv stands for "list server." With Listserv software, incoming e-mail messages can be forwarded quickly to the thousands of e-mail addresses on a mailing list. Anyone with an interest in a particular topic can put his or her name on a mailing list. Anyone wanting to send a message regarding the topic of the mailing list sends it to the list server, which immediately forwards the message to all subscribers.

Some e-mail lists are public, which means they are open to anyone. Others are private, which means you must be approved by a moderator in order to join the list. Subscribing—or unsubscribing—to a mailing list involves sending an e-mail message to the computer that maintains the list. Once you have subscribed, every message sent to the list server will be sent to you. If you send a message to the list server, it will be sent to all subscribers, including you. The activity level for different mailing lists can vary greatly. Some mailing lists may generate a couple of messages a month; others could generate hundreds of messages a week.

steps

1. Connect to your Internet Service Provider. Then click the Outlook Express button on the Taskbar. If necessary, click the *Inbox* folder.

2. Click the New Mail button ![New Mail] .

3. In the To box, key **listserv@PEACH.EASE.LSOFT.COM**. Leave the Subject box blank.

   You are subscribing to a mailing list called "The Microsoft Excel Developers List," which serves as a forum for users of Microsoft Excel.

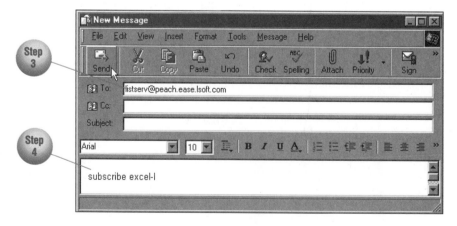

4. In the body of the message, key **subscribe excel-l**.

5 Generally, you do not want a signature in the message sent to subscribe to a mailing list. To delete your signature, move the mouse pointer so that it is before the first letter in your name. Click and drag to highlight your entire signature. Then press the Delete key.

6 Click the Send button. When the dialog box appears warning you that the message has no subject, click OK.

Whenever you subscribe to a mailing list you receive an e-mail message confirming your request to join the mailing list.

7 After waiting a few minutes, click the Send/Recv button to see if you receive the confirmation e-mail.

If the message still has not arrived after you have clicked the Send/Recv button a couple of times, you may need to return to this exercise at a later time.

8 For this particular mailing list, you will receive an e-mail message saying you must reply to it within 48 hours to be added to the list. When you receive this message, click it once in the Message list to select it, click the Reply button and in the message area, key **ok**.

9 Click the Send button.

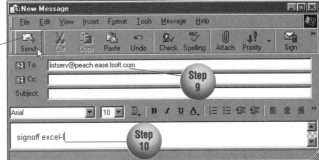

You will receive an e-mail confirming that you are subscribed to the list. Read this e-mail carefully as it explains how to send messages to the list and how to cancel your subscription (print and save these instructions).

10 To unsubscribe from the list, click the New Mail button. In the To box, key **listserv@peach.ease.lsoft.com**. Do not enter anything in the Subject box.

11 In the message area, key **signoff excel-l**. Then delete your signature at the bottom of the message.

12 Click the Send button. When the dialog box appears warning you that the message has no subject, click OK.

13 Click the Close button **X** in the upper right corner of the Outlook Express window to close Outlook Express.

14 Follow the correct procedures to disconnect from your Internet Service Provider.

Finding Mailing Lists of Interest

You can find a public mailing list for nearly every topic imaginable. Several Web sites maintain lists of public mailing lists. Consider visiting the following Web sites and browsing through their extensive indexes of available public mailing lists:

http://www.liszt.com/
http://tile.net/listserv/index.html
http://paml.alastra.com/

Subscribing to Newsgroups

One very popular use of the Internet is for discussion groups. A newsgroup is a discussion group that provides participants a forum for sharing information on a particular topic. Newsgroups are set up by subject matter, and the name of the newsgroup describes the particular subject discussed. Newsgroups are organized by categories. Some of the main categories are biz (business), comp (computers), rec (recreation), sci (science), and soc (social). Each main category has several subcategories under it. In the newsgroup name, the categories are separated from one another by periods. For example, the newsgroup *rec.photo.equipment.35mm* carries messages in the main category of recreation, more specifically in photography, more specifically in photographic equipment, and even more specifically in photographic equipment related to 35mm cameras. Subscribers receive via e-mail all messages posted to the newsgroup.

steps

① Connect to your Internet Service Provider. Click the Outlook Express button on the Taskbar.

② Click your news server, which should be the last folder in the Folders list.

The name of the news server folder will vary according to the news server you use.

③ If you are not subscribed to any newsgroups, a dialog box is displayed asking if you want to view a list of the available newsgroups. Click <u>Y</u>es.

The Newsgroup Subscriptions window is displayed. The topics are listed in alphabetical order.

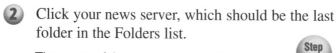

 Problem

If the dialog box does not appear, click the Newsgroups button 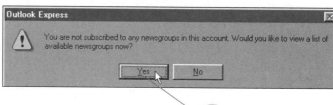.

④ You want to find a newsgroup about dogs. In the <u>D</u>isplay newsgroups which contain box, which appears at the top of the window, key **dogs**.

Newsgroups containing the word *dogs* are displayed.

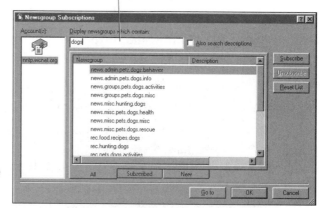

(5) Find the newsgroup called rec.pets.dogs.behavior and double-click it.

An icon appears to the left of the newsgroup name, indicating that you have subscribed to that newsgroup.

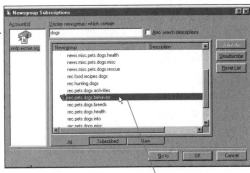

(6) Find the newsgroup called rec.pets.dogs.breeds and double-click it.

An icon appears to the left of the newsgroup name, indicating that you have subscribed to that newsgroup.

Step 5

Problem

?

If you cannot find the newsgroup rec.pets.dogs.behavior, it may not be available on your particular news server. If so, double-click an available newsgroup related to dogs.

(7) To display the entire newsgroup list again, double-click the word *dogs* in the <u>D</u>isplay newsgroups that contain box and then press the Delete key.

(8) Key **newusers** in the <u>D</u>isplay newsgroups which contain box.

Newsgroups containing the word *newusers* are displayed.

(9) Find the newsgroup news.newusers.questions and double-click it.

An icon appears to the left of the newsgroup name, indicating that you have subscribed to that newsgroup.

(10) To display the entire newsgroup list again, double-click the word *newusers* in the <u>D</u>isplay newsgroups that contain box and press the Delete key.

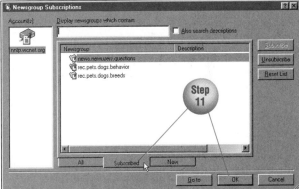

Step 11

(11) Click the Subscribed tab to see a list of all of the newsgroups to which you subscribed.

(12) Click OK.

The newsgroups you subscribed to are now listed in the Folders list under the news server. If you cannot see a list of the newsgroups, click the plus sign next to the news server. The plus sign turns into a minus sign and all of the newsgroups are displayed.

(13) You decide you no longer want to subscribe to the rec.pets.dog.breeds newsgroup. To unsubscribe, right-click the newsgroup name in the Folders list. Then click <u>U</u>nsubscribe in the shortcut menu that displays.

(14) When the warning box asking if you are sure that you want to unsubscribe from this newsgroup appears, click OK.

The newsgroup is deleted from the Folders list.

(15) Click the Close button **X** in the upper right corner of the Outlook Express window to close Outlook Express. Then disconnect from your Internet Service Provider.

Reading
Newsgroup Messages

Once you have subscribed to a newsgroup, you can read any of the messages posted to it. These messages give the advice, opinions, ideas, and suggestions of people from various locations around the world. Posting a new message can start a *thread*. A thread includes a main message and the messages posted as a reply to that particular message. Newsgroup subscribers can review all of the current messages in a thread. A plus sign next to a message indicates it is part of a thread. Before you can read the messages in a newsgroup, you need to download them to your computer by double-clicking the newsgroup name. Depending on the topic and the activity in the newsgroup, hundreds of new messages may be posted every day, or there may be only a couple of new messages posted every few weeks. Remember that some newsgroups are unmonitored, which means that no one reads the messages before they are posted. If you find some messages offensive, simply unsubscribe from that newsgroup.

steps

1. Connect to your Internet Service Provider and access Outlook Express. Then click the news server.

2. Double-click the newsgroup called *news.newusers.questions*.

   A list of the newsgroup's messages appears in the Message list.

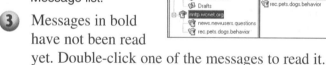

3. Messages in bold have not been read yet. Double-click one of the messages to read it.

   The message is displayed in its own window.

4. Once you have read the message, click the Close button 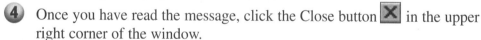 in the upper right corner of the window.

5. Choose a message that has a thread (indicated by a plus sign). Click the plus sign.

   The plus sign becomes a minus sign, and all of the replies to that message are displayed below it.

6 Double-click the first message in the thread to read it. Then click the Next button to display the next message.

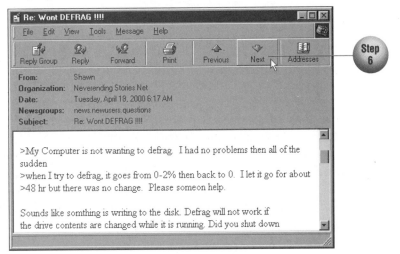

7 Click the Previous button Previous to display the previous message.

8 Click the Next button to read all of the messages in the thread. When you have read all of the messages, click the Close button ✖ in the upper right corner of the window to close the message.

9 Read through any other threads in the newsgroup of interest to you.

10 Click the Close button ✖ in the upper right corner of the Outlook Express window to close Outlook Express. Then disconnect from your Internet Service Provider.

Take 2

FAQs

If you decide to participate in a newsgroup, chances are you will soon have some basic questions about the topic. People who participate in newsgroups on a regular basis get tired of answering these same questions over and over each time a new person joins the group. For this reason, many newsgroups include an "FAQ," which stands for "Frequently Asked Questions." An FAQ is a message that contains a list of the most commonly asked questions and their answers. Whenever you join a newsgroup, check for an FAQ and read it. Newsgroup participants become very annoyed when people post messages asking questions that have already been answered in the FAQ. The news.answers newsgroup contains a number of FAQs for a variety of newsgroups.

Posting New Messages

Before posting messages to newsgroups, you should understand a few rules of appropriate behavior. Most of these rules simply involve being considerate. For example, you should never publicly embarrass or insult another user. If you do insult others publicly, your own reputation will be damaged and this could be very detrimental to your Internet communications. A common suggestion is that new users "lurk" in the background for a while before they join in the discussion. Lurking means to read all of the messages without posting any yourself. Lurking gives you a sense of the type of message that is appropriate for the newsgroup as well as which topics have been exhausted. Keep your messages short and to-the-point. Do not post messages that simply agree with what has already been said. If you do not have something new to add, do not post anything. Messages can either be posted to the entire newsgroup or they can be posted to an individual member. Personal messages should not be posted to the newsgroup as a whole. When replying to a message, ask yourself whether or not everyone in the newsgroup would be interested in reading what you have to say. If the message is primarily of interest to a specific person, send an e-mail message to that particular person.

steps

1. Connect to your Internet Service Provider and access Outlook Express. Then click your news server.

   The Newsgroup Subscriptions window is displayed.

2. Click the Newsgroup button Newsgroups... .

3. In the Display newsgroups which contain box, key **alt.test**.

4. The alt.test newsgroup provides an area where people can post a test message. Click *alt.test* to select the newsgroup.

5. Click the Subscribe button. Then click OK.

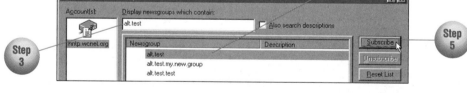

6. In the Folders list, double-click *alt.test* to download the messages.

7. Make sure the alt.test newsgroup is selected in the Folders list. Then click the New Post button.

   A new post window is displayed.

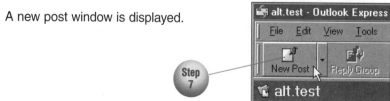

8 In the Subject box, key your last name followed by the word **test**.

9 In the message area, key the following: **This is the first message I have posted to a newsgroup. This is a test to see if I can do it correctly**. Then click the Send button.

10 At the information box that displays saying your message may not appear immediately, click OK.

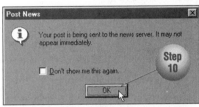

11 Now you want to check to see if your message was posted to the newsgroup. To download the message, click Tools, then Get Next 300 Headers.

12 Look for your message. If you do not find it right away, click Edit, point to Find, and click Message.

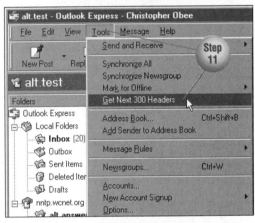

13 At the Find Message window, enter your last name and the word **test** in the Subject box.

14 Click Find Now.

Your post should be listed at the bottom of the window.

15 Click the Close button ☒ in the upper right corner of the Find Message window.

16 Close Outlook Express and disconnect from your Internet Service Provider.

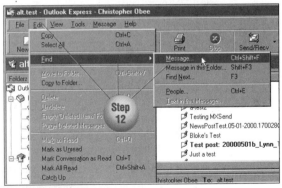

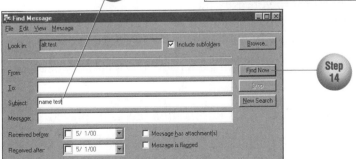

Replying to an Existing Newsgroup Message

Typically, people reply to newsgroup messages to answer a question, express an opinion, or offer additional information. You can reply either to the author of the message only or to the entire newsgroup. Remember, you should reply to a message only if you have something important to contribute. Simply agreeing with something someone else has said is not a useful contribution to any discussion. To reply to a message, click that message in the Message list. If you want to reply to the author only, click the Reply button on the toolbar. If you want to reply to the entire newsgroup, click the Reply Group button on the toolbar. The appropriate recipient e-mail address is automatically displayed in the To box, and you can compose and send the message.

steps

1 Connect to your Internet Service Provider and access Outlook Express. Then click your news server.

2 Click the *alt.test* folder in the Folders list.

3 In the Message list, find the test message you sent to the alt.test newsgroup and click it once to select it.

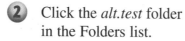

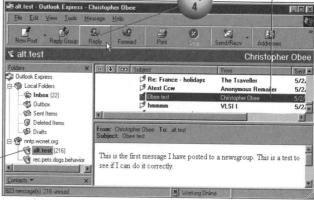

 Problem ? Can't find the test message you sent to the alt.test newsgroup? Repeat the exercise in the previous section, "Posting New Messages."

4 First you will send a message replying to the author only. Click the Reply button.

5 At the message window that displays, note by the address in the To box that the message is being sent to you. Key the following: **This message is a reply to the author only.**

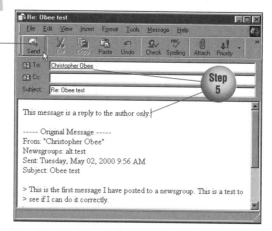

If necessary, scroll down the window to see the copy of the original message.

6 Click Send.

7 When the Post News information box is displayed, click OK.

8 In the Folders list, click the *Inbox* to check if the message was sent to you.

(9) Click the Send/Recv button 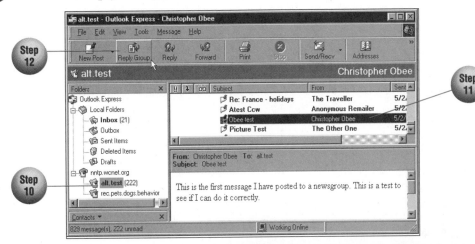 .

You should receive the message you just sent.

(10) Next you want to practice sending a reply message that goes to the entire newsgroup. In the Folders list, click the *alt.test* folder.

(11) In the Messages list, click your test message to select it.

(12) Click the Reply Group button.

(13) At the message window that displays, note by the address in the To box that the message is being sent to the entire newsgroup. Key the following: **This reply is being sent to the entire newsgroup.**

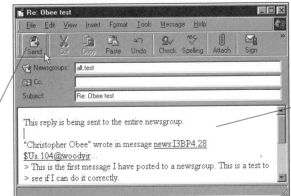

(14) Click the Send button.

(15) When the Post News information box is displayed, click OK.

(16) To check if your reply was posted to the newsgroup, download new messages by clicking Tools, then Get Next 300 Headers.

A plus sign should appear next to your original message, indicating there is now a reply to that message.

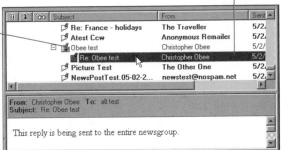

(17) Click the plus sign to display the reply.

The plus sign changes to a minus sign.

(18) Click the message you sent as a reply to the entire newsgroup.

Your message is displayed in the Preview pane.

(19) Close Outlook Express and disconnect from your Internet Service Provider.

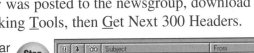

Features Summary

Feature	Button	Menu	Keyboard
Attach a file to a message	Attach	Insert, File Attachment	
Close Outlook Express	X	File, Close	
Create a new message	New Mail	Message, New Message	Ctrl + N
Create a Signature		Tools, Options	
Delete a message	Delete	Edit, Delete	Ctrl + D
Display the next message in a newsgroup thread	Next	View, Next, Next Message	Ctrl + >
Display the previous message in a newsgroup thread	Previous	View, Previous Message	Ctrl + <
Launch Outlook Express			
Post a newsgroup message	New Post	File, New, News Message	
Print a message	Print	File, Print	Ctrl + P
Reply to everyone in a newsgroup	Reply Group	Message, Reply to Group	Ctrl + G
Reply to the author and anyone else to whom the message was sent	Reply All	Message, Reply to All	Ctrl + Shift + R
Reply to the author of an e-mail message or a newsgroup message	Reply	Message, Reply to Sender	Ctrl + R
Send all outgoing messages and receive any new mail	Send/Recv	Tools, Send and Receive, Send and Receive All	Ctrl + M
Send an e-mail message to the recipient	Send	File, Send Message	Alt + S

Procedures Check

In the space provided at the right, indicate the correct term, icon, button, or command.

1. This is the name for a network of computers that exchange articles called newsgroups. _____

2. This is what the number in brackets to the right of the *Inbox* folder indicates. _____

3. This icon displays in the Message list next to each unread e-mail message. _____

4. Click this option on the Tools menu in order to create a signature. _____

5. In an e-mail address, this is the abbreviation for an educational institution. _____

6. If you want to send a copy of an e-mail message to someone else besides the main recipient, enter the e-mail address of the person who is to receive the copy in this box. _____

7. Copies of the e-mail messages you send are stored in this folder. _____

8. Click this button if you want to check for new e-mail messages. _____

9. Press this button to send an e-mail message to the person whose e-mail message to you is currently selected. _____

10. Click this button if you want to send a Word document or Excel spreadsheet along with an e-mail button. _____

11. If a message has a file attached to it, this icon appears in the upper right corner of the Preview pane for that message. _____

12. The name of a file that is attached to an e-mail message appears in this box. _____

13. This is the kind of software that manages mailing lists. _____

14. This is where you must send an e-mail message that you want to join a mailing list. _____

15. If the name of a newsgroup includes this abbreviation, the discussions in the newsgroup focus on games, hobbies, and other recreational topics. _____

16. To access newsgroups, you must select this folder in the Folders list. _____

17. This term refers to a main message in a newsgroup along with any of the messages that have been posted as a reply to that particular message. _____

18. If a message in the Message list has this symbol next to it, there are replies to that message that currently are not displayed. _____

19. This term refers to people who frequently read the messages in a newsgroup but do not post a message. _____

20. If you want to send a reply only to the author of a newsgroup message and not to the entire newsgroup at large, click this button. _____

Skills Review

Activity 1: Creating and Sending E-Mail

1 Exchange e-mail addresses with another member of your class.
2 Connect to the Internet and access Outlook Express.
3 Click the New Mail button.
4 In the To box, enter your classmate's e-mail address.
5 In the Cc box, enter your e-mail address.
6 Enter **Activity 1** in the Subject box.
7 In the message area, enter a brief message regarding what you like best about using e-mail.
8 Click the Send button.
9 After a few moments, click the Send/Recv button to receive the copy of the message you sent to yourself.
10 Select the copy of the message.
11 Click the Print button.
12 Close Outlook Express.
13 Disconnect from the Internet.

Activity 2: Reading and Responding to E-Mail

1 Connect to the Internet and access Outlook Express.
2 If necessary, click the Send/Recv button to receive any new e-mail.
3 Find the message that your classmate sent to you with *Activity 1* for a subject. Double-click the message to open it.
4 Read the message. Click the Print button to print the message.
5 Click the Reply button.
6 In the message area, write a brief message thanking your classmate for sending you the message.

7   Click the Send button.
8   Find the copy of the message you sent to yourself in Activity 1 and click it to select it.
9   Click the Delete button.
10 Click the *Deleted Items* folder. The message you just deleted should be in the folder.
11 Right-click the *Deleted Items* folder and then click Empty 'Deleted Items Folder.'
12 When the warning box is displayed, click the Yes button.
13 Close Outlook Express.
14 Disconnect from the Internet.

Activity 3: Attaching a File to a Message

1   Exchange e-mail addresses with a classmate.
2   From the Start menu, point to Programs, point to Accessories, and click Notepad.
3   In the Notepad window, enter a brief message regarding the features in Windows 98 with which you are so comfortable that you would be willing to teach them to another student.
4   Click File and Save.
5   Save the file on the Desktop using the file name Win 98.
6   Close Notepad.
7   Connect to the Internet and access Outlook Express.
8   Click the New Mail button.
9   In the To box, enter your classmate's e-mail address.
10 In the Cc box, enter your e-mail address.
11 Enter **Win 98 Attachment** in the Subject box.
12 In the message area, enter a brief message stating that the attached file lists the features of Windows 98 in which you feel skilled enough to help out someone else who is having difficulty in those areas.
13 Click the Attach button.
14 Navigate to the Win 98 file on the desktop and click it to select it.
15 Click the Attach button.
16 Click the Send button.
17 Close Outlook Express.
18 Disconnect from the Internet.

Activity 4: Opening an Attachment

1   Connect to the Internet and access Outlook Express.
2   If necessary, click the Send/Recv button to receive any new e-mail messages.
3   Find the message that your classmate sent to you with *Win 98 Attachment* for a subject. Double-click the message to open it.
4   Click the Attachment button in the upper right corner of the Preview pane. Click the file name *Win 98.txt*.
5   In the Open Attachment window, click the Open it option and then click OK.
6   Print the Win 98 file.
7   Close the Win 98 file.
8   Close Outlook Express.
9   Disconnect from the Internet.

Activity 5: Subscribing to Newsgroups

1 Connect to the Internet and access Outlook Express.
2 Click your news server folder.
3 Click the Newsgroups button.
4 Key **movies current** in the <u>D</u>isplay newsgroups which contain box.
5 Find the newsgroup rec.arts.movies.current-films. Double-click it to subscribe to it.
6 Click OK.
7 To see the messages in the newsgroup rec.arts.movies.current-films, double-click its name in the Folders list.
8 Find a subject line that interests you and double-click it to open that message.
9 Click the Print button.
10 Close the message.
11 Close Outlook Express.
12 Disconnect from the Internet.

Activity 6: Unsubscribing from Newsgroups

1 Connect to the Internet and access Outlook Express.
2 If a plus sign is displayed next to your news server folder, click it so that all of the newsgroups to which you are subscribed are displayed.
3 Right-click the newsgroup *rec.arts.movies.current-films* and click <u>U</u>nsubscribe.
4 When the warning box appears, click OK.
5 Close Outlook Express.
6 Disconnect from the Internet.

Performance Plus

Activity 1: Sending E-Mail

1 Connect to the Internet and access Outlook Express.
2 Send an e-mail message to a friend that outlines all of the things you learned to do using Outlook Express. Enter your e-mail address in the Cc box.
3 After a few moments, check your e-mail to receive the copy of the message you sent to yourself.
4 Print a copy of the message you sent to yourself.
5 Close Outlook Express.
6 Disconnect from the Internet.

Activity 2: Subscribing to Mailing Lists

1 Connect to the Internet and access Internet Explorer.
2 Go to the following URL: http://tile.net/listserv/index.html.
3 Browse this Web site until you find a mailing list in which you are interested.
4 Subscribe to a mailing list that interests you by following the directions that are provided.
5 Print the page that gives the directions on how to unsubscribe from the mailing list. File this page in a safe place.
6 Close Internet Explorer.
7 You may have to wait a few days, but once you have received a message from the mailing list, print it.
8 If you decide to unsubscribe from the mailing list after reading several messages, use the directions on the page you printed in step 5 to unsubscribe from the list.

Activity 3: Subscribing to Newsgroups

1 Connect to the Internet and access Outlook Express.
2 Click your news server folder. Click the Newsgroups button.
3 Browse through the newsgroups available from your news server. Find a couple of newsgroups that interest you and subscribe to them.
4 Access the messages for each of the newsgroups to which you subscribed.
5 Read several of the messages and pick one of them to print.
6 If you find a message to which you have a meaningful response, send a reply to that message. If you send a reply to the entire newsgroup, print a copy of your reply when it appears in the newsgroup.
7 If, after reading the messages in the newsgroups, you decide you are not interested in that newsgroup, unsubscribe from it.
8 Close Outlook Express.
9 Disconnect from the Internet.

Activity 4: Finding Information on How to Create an Address Book

1   Connect to the Internet and access Outlook Express.
2   Use the Help feature in Outlook Express to learn how to open the Address Book, how to add a contact to the Address Book, and how to send messages from the Address Book. Take notes on how to do these three things.
3   Using what you just learned, add the e-mail addresses of at least two of your friends and/or family members to your Address Book.
4   Send an e-mail message to a friend/family member by retrieving his or her e-mail address from your Address Book.
5   Close Outlook Express.
6   Disconnect from the Internet.

Activity 5: Attaching a File to an E-Mail Message

1   Using Notepad, write the directions for how to open the Address Book, how to add a contact to the Address Book, and how to send messages from the Address Book. You took notes on how to do these procedures in step 2 of Activity 4. Save and then print the file.
2   Send an e-mail message to a friend who might be interested in learning how to use the Address Book in Outlook Express. Attach the file you created in step 1 to the e-mail message.

Maintaining and Optimizing the Computer

We all take for granted the many things we can do so effortlessly with the computer. Computers seem to work flawlessly—until a disaster strikes. Your floppy disk with your only copy of a report that is due in two hours suddenly has some kind of disk error that makes all the data inaccessible. The hard disk on your computer fails. The hard disk is full and you cannot store any more data on it. Unfortunately, there is a long list of things that can go wrong with your computer. The good news is that many of those things are preventable with the proper maintenance of your computer.

Just as you would not expect a car to run perfectly without any maintenance, you should not expect your computer to run well without maintenance. Windows 98 includes many tools to help you maintain your computer so that it operates at peak performance. The Maintenance Wizard, for example, makes your programs run faster, checks your hard disk for problems, and frees up hard disk space. The Disk Defragmenter rearranges files and unused space on your hard disk so that programs run faster. ScanDisk checks your hard disk for physical errors and then repairs any damaged areas it finds. DriveSpace frees up space on your hard drive by compressing files. Disk Cleanup scans the hard drive for files that are no longer needed and can be deleted safely. The Windows Components feature enables you to add or remove software on your hard drive.

Maintaining your data files is equally important. You should always have an extra copy, or a backup, of any file you create. Make backup copies of files stored on a floppy disk as well as files stored on a hard drive.

Many of the Windows maintenance tools—Disk Defragmenter, for example—can be set up so they are performed automatically at a set time period. Setting these tools to run automatically helps to ensure that you will maintain your computer on a regular basis. Performing maintenance routines may not guarantee your system will run flawlessly 100 percent of the time. But it definitely will help prevent many potential problems from occurring as well as ensure that your computer is set up for optimal performance. In this section, you will learn the following skills:

Skills

- Display disk and system properties
- Use Disk Cleanup
- Use ScanDisk
- Use Disk Defragmenter
- Use Data Compression
- Use the Maintenance Wizard
- Back up data files on the hard drive
- Restore a backup
- Make a backup copy of a floppy disk
- Create a startup disk

Displaying Disk Properties

Basic information about a disk—either your hard disk or a floppy disk—such as its size and how much space is available on it can be easily located and displayed. Say, for example, you want to install a new program on your hard disk. Before you install the program, you may want to know how much space is available. The Windows 98 Properties command provides you with this information.

steps

1. Double-click the *My Computer* icon.

2. Right-click the icon for the hard disk drive. (On most systems the hard disk drive is labeled (C:).)

3. From the shortcut menu that is displayed, click Properties.

4. At the Properties window that displays, locate the amount of used space and free space on the disk.

5. Locate the total amount of space available on the disk.

6. Click OK to close the Properties window.

7. Insert a floppy disk into the floppy disk drive.

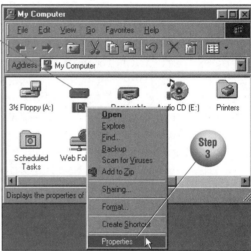

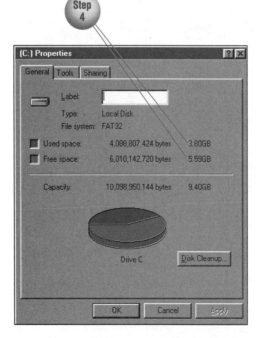

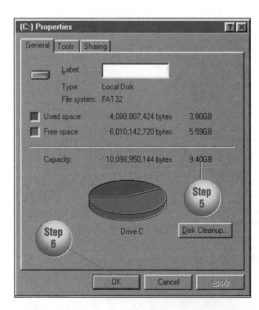

⑧ Right-click the icon for the floppy disk drive. (On most systems the floppy disk drive is labeled 3½ Floppy (A:).)

⑨ From the shortcut menu that displays, click Properties.

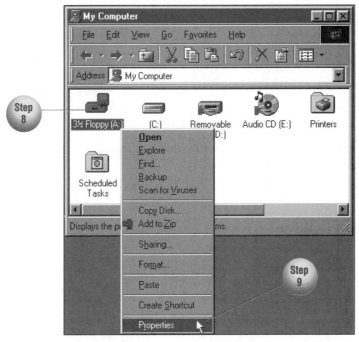

⑩ At the Properties window that displays, locate the amount of used space and free space on the disk.

⑪ Locate the total amount of space available on the disk.

⑫ Click OK to close the Properties window.

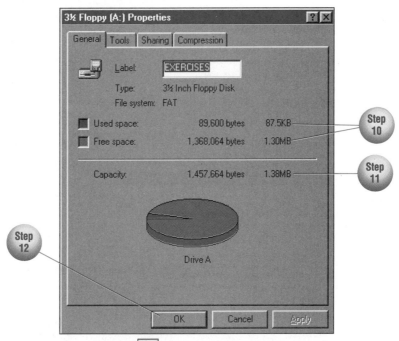

⑬ Click the Close button ⊠ in the upper right corner to close the My Computer window.

Using Disk Cleanup

The purpose of the Windows 98 Disk Cleanup tool is to free up space on your hard disk drive by deleting unnecessary files. Disk Cleanup deletes several different types of files, including temporary files and files that have been placed in the Recycle Bin. When you use the World Wide Web, for example, Web pages sometimes are stored on your computer so that they can be accessed quickly. Once you have finished viewing the Web page, these temporary files are no longer necessary and can be deleted. Some programs create files for storing temporary information. Once the file is closed, this temporary information is no longer needed but may remain on the hard drive. These unnecessary files clutter up your hard disk drive, taking up valuable space. Periodically, they should be removed using Disk Cleanup.

steps

1 Click the Start button on the Taskbar, point to Programs, point to Accessories, point to System Tools, and then click Disk Cleanup.

The Select Drive window is displayed. This window enables you to select the disk drive you want to clean up. The default is drive C:.

2 With the icon for drive C displayed in the Drives box, click OK.

After a few moments, the Disk Cleanup for (C:) window is displayed. The Files to delete box displays the types of files that can be deleted and how much space each type of file is taking up on your disk. When you select an option in the Files to delete box, a description of that type of file is displayed in the Description box. If you want to view the individual files that have been selected for removal, select one of the options in the Files to delete box by clicking it and then click the View Files button toward the bottom of the screen.

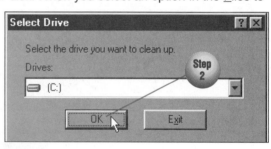

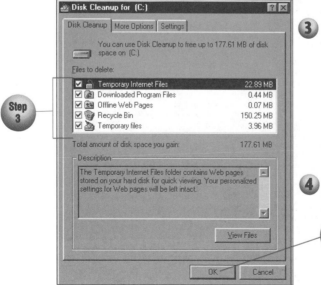

3 Make sure there is a checkmark in the boxes next to each type of file. If there is not a checkmark, click that box to select it.

Disk Cleanup deletes only the files indicated by a checkmark in the box next to the type of file.

4 Click OK.

x

⑤ When the window is displayed asking if you are sure you want to delete files, click <u>Y</u>es.

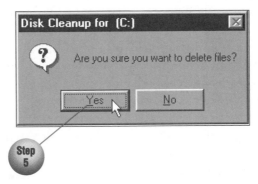

⑥ A window is displayed that reports the progress of Disk Cleanup. When all the files have been deleted, the window disappears and you are at the Windows desktop.

Using Troubleshooters

Windows 98 Help includes a Help feature called Troubleshooters that can be very useful if you are having a problem with your hardware or software. Troubleshooters can help you diagnose common problems and suggest ways to fix them. To access a troubleshooter in Windows 98 Help, click Start on the Taskbar and then click Help. Click the <u>C</u>ontents tab, click Troubleshooting, click Windows 98 Troubleshooters, and then click the topic you want.

> Click the <u>C</u>ontents tab, click Troubleshooting, click Windows 98 Troubleshooters, and then from the list of topics that is displayed, click the topic you want.

Using ScanDisk

The ScanDisk utility helps you fix problems you may encounter with your hard disk, such as problems caused by physical damage to the surface or damaged storage areas. Problems can develop in various situations. For example, when you shut down your computer by clicking the Start button on the Taskbar and then clicking Shut Down, Windows 98 performs several internal checks to make sure programs and files are closed and stored properly. If the system is shut down without those internal checks being made, certain locations on the disk may become unusable. Scratches or other physical harm are another type of disk problem. ScanDisk checks your hard disk drive for storage errors as well as for physical damage. If it finds any problems, it then tries to fix them.

steps

1 Click the Start button on the Taskbar, point to Programs, point to Accessories, point to System Tools, and then click ScanDisk.

The ScanDisk window is displayed. The default disk drive to be scanned is disk drive (C:).

2 Make sure drive C: is selected. If it is not, click it to select it.

Two types of tests can be performed, Standard and Thorough. The Standard option checks the files and folders on the selected drive for errors. The Thorough option checks the files and folders on the selected drive for errors and checks the physical integrity of the disk's surface. As a rule, try the Standard option first. If you still encounter problems with your hard disk drive, try the Thorough option.

3 Make sure the Standard option is selected. If it is not, click it to select it.

4 Make sure the Automatically fix errors box is selected. If it is not, click it to select it.

If the Automatically fix errors option is selected, Windows 98 will automatically fix any errors it finds. If this option is not selected, each time Windows 98 encounters an error it will stop and a dialog box will be displayed asking if you want to fix the particular error it found.

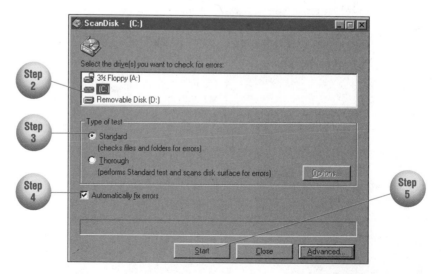

(5) Click <u>S</u>tart.

As ScanDisk checks the hard disk drive, its progress is displayed at the bottom of the ScanDisk window

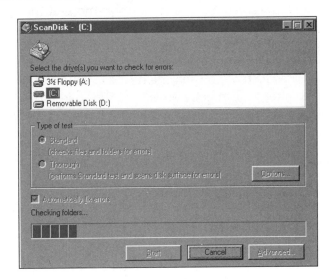

(6) When the scan is complete, the ScanDisk Results window is displayed. Click the Close button.

This window reports whether or not ScanDisk found any errors. It also reports on the files stored on the hard disk drive.

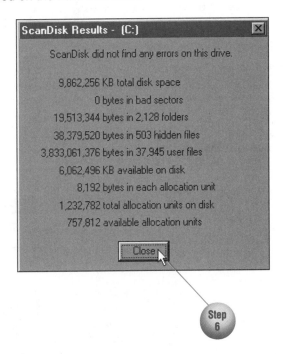

(7) Click the Close button in the ScanDisk window.

Using
Disk Defragmenter

A file is saved on a disk in storage locations called *clusters*. The computer saves part of a file in one cluster, moves on to the next available cluster and stores more of the file, moves on to the next available cluster and stores more of the file, and so on until the entire file has been saved. Ideally, the clusters that store all the data for one file should be contiguous, or right next to one another, on the drive. But as more files are saved to a drive and deleted from a drive, that becomes impossible. The computer saves a file in one cluster and then the next available cluster may be on another part of the disk. The cluster available after that may be on yet another part of the disk. As the file is saved, it is fragmented, that is, stored in noncontiguous clusters. A fragmented file may take longer to access because the computer has to search many different parts of the drive in order to retrieve it. The more fragmented a drive becomes, the more likely you are to lose data on your drive. Windows 98 Disk Defragmenter finds all the fragmented parts of a file and moves them so they are all stored in clusters next to one another on the disk.

steps

① Click the Start button, point to <u>P</u>rograms, point to Accessories, point to System Tools, and then click Disk Defragmenter.

The Select Drive window is displayed. Defragmenting a disk can take hours. Generally, it is a good idea to back up a drive before defragmenting it. You will learn how to back up the hard drive later on in this section.

② Make sure drive C: is selected. If it is not, click it to select it. Then check with your instructor before clicking OK to begin the defragmentation process.

If you click OK, the Deframenting Drive C window is displayed. This window keeps track of the defragmentation progress. Note the three buttons on the window. The defragmentation process can be stopped at any time by clicking the <u>S</u>top button. If you click the <u>S</u>top button, however, the process has to start all over again from the beginning. Clicking the <u>P</u>ause button stops the process temporarily, meaning if you click the <u>R</u>esume button, the process will pick up from where it left off.

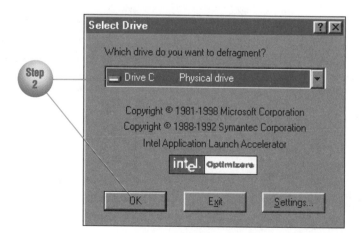

3 Click the Show Details button (assuming you launched the defragmenting process).

A visual representation of the computer's rearranging the clusters is displayed. Each little box represents a cluster.

4 Click the Legend button.

The Defrag Legend window is displayed. This window identifies what each differently colored square represents.

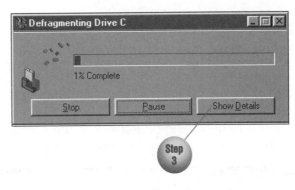

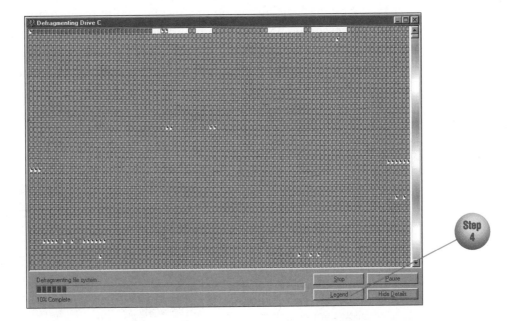

5 Click the Close button.

6 When the defragmentation process is completed, a window is displayed notifying you that the disk has been defragmented. Click Yes to close this window.

7 If the (C:) Properties window is still displayed, click the Cancel button.

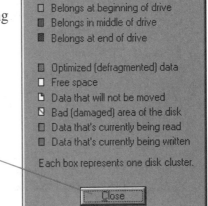

Using the Maintenance Wizard

The Windows 98 Maintenance Wizard is a tool designed to remove unnecessary files, make your programs run faster, and check your hard disk for problems, optimizing the performance of your computer. The Maintenance Wizard combines ScanDisk, Disk Cleanup, Disk Defragmenter, and other tools into one convenient feature. You can use the wizard to schedule these utilities to run automatically on a regular basis, during periods when the computer is not in use. Scheduling the utilities to run on a routine basis helps to ensure that your computer will consistently perform at its best.

steps

1. Click the Start button on the Taskbar, point to Programs, point to Accessories, point to System Tools, and then click Maintenance Wizard.

   The first Maintenance Wizard dialog box is displayed. Read the description of the Maintenance. The Express option uses the most common maintenance settings.

Problem?

If maintenance settings have alreaady been established for your computer, a dialog box may appear asking if you want to perform maintenance now or change the current settings. Select the Change my maintenance settings now option and click OK.

2. Make sure the Express option is selected. Then click Next.

   The second Maintenance Wizard dialog box is displayed. This window allows you to select when the maintenance tasks will be performed.

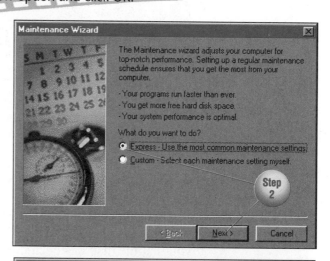

3. Make sure the Nights – Midnight to 3:00 AM option is selected. Then click Next.

   The third, and final, Maintenance Wizard dialog box is displayed. This window displays the three tasks that will be performed, which are Disk Defragmenter, ScanDisk, and Disk Cleanup.

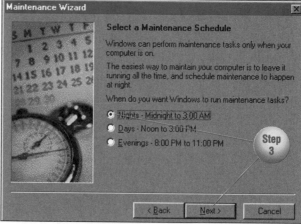

④ Clicking the Finish button would finish scheduling the maintenance tasks. Then, provided your computer was turned on, those tasks would automatically be performed at the time scheduled. For the purposes of this exercise, click the Cancel button to cancel scheduling the maintenance tasks.

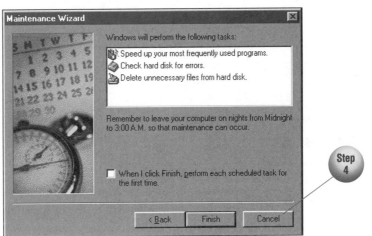

Step 4

The Task Scheduler

Take 2

Another way to automatically schedule routine maintenance tasks is with the Task Scheduler. The Task Scheduler gives you more control over scheduling maintenance utilities than is provided with the Maintenance Wizard. The Task Scheduler enables you to schedule a task to run daily, weekly, monthly, or at certain times—such as when you first start the computer. You can also change the schedule for a task, stop a scheduled task, or customize how a task runs at a scheduled time using the Task Scheduler.

To access the Task Scheduler, double-click the *My Computer* icon. Then, from the My Computer window, double-click the *Scheduled Tasks* folder, as shown in Figure WIN5-1. The Scheduled Tasks window is displayed. To add tasks, double-click Add Scheduled Task, as shown in Figure WIN5-2.

FIGURE WIN5.1 Accessing the Task Scheduler

The Scheduled Task Wizard is started. Follow the directions provided by the Scheduled Task Wizard to schedule maintenance tasks. The Task Scheduler also enables you to modify, delete, pause, or stop the tasks that you have already scheduled. In addition to maintenance tasks, this feature of Windows 98 can be used to schedule any application to run.

FIGURE WIN5.2 Starting the Scheduled Task Wizard

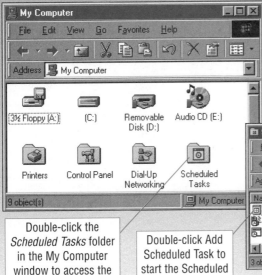

Double-click the *Scheduled Tasks* folder in the My Computer window to access the Task Scheduler.

Double-click Add Scheduled Task to start the Scheduled Task Wizard.

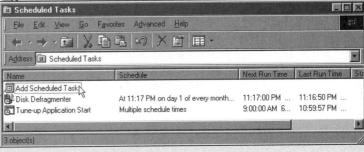

Backing Up Data Files on a Hard Disk Drive

You should always have *backups*, or extra copies, of all your files, whether they are on the hard disk drive or on floppy disks. That way, if something happens to the original files, you can restore them from the backup copies. The importance of having backup copies of files cannot be overemphasized. Unfortunately, most people do not take this advice seriously—that is, until a crucial file is lost or damaged and they are stuck without a backup copy. The Backup feature in Windows 98 can be used to back up files on your hard disk to another storage medium such as floppy disks, a tape drive, or another computer on the network. The first time you back up files on the hard disk drive, back up all the files. This gives you a complete copy of the entire hard disk drive. Subsequently, you only need to back up the files that have changed since the last time the disk was backed up.

steps

(Note: You will need a floppy disk to complete the following exercise. Before completing the steps, make sure the Windows Data Files *folder and its contents are available on your computer's hard drive. This folder can be downloaded from the EMC/Paradigm Web site, or you may get it from your instructor.)*

1 Click the Start button on the Taskbar, point to Programs, point to Accessories, point to System Tools, and then click Backup.

A welcome window providing an explanation of the meaning of "backup" is displayed.

Problem

? If the Backup option is not available on the System Tools menu, it probably has not been installed from the Windows 98 CD-ROM. Check with your instructor or network manager.

2 Make sure the Create a new backup job option is selected. Then click OK.

The first window in the Backup Wizard is displayed. If the files on the hard disk drive have never been backed up, you would want to back up all the files. For the purposes of this exercise, you will back up only selected files.

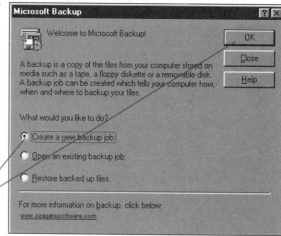

Step 2

3 Click the Back up selected files, folders, and drives option. Then click Next.

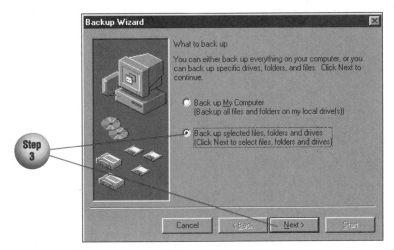

4 Locate the *Windows Data Files* folder on your computer's hard drive. Then click the box next to that folder to select it. (There should be a blue checkmark in the box.)

5 Click Next.

The third window in the Backup Wizard is displayed. This window allows you to specify which files to back up.

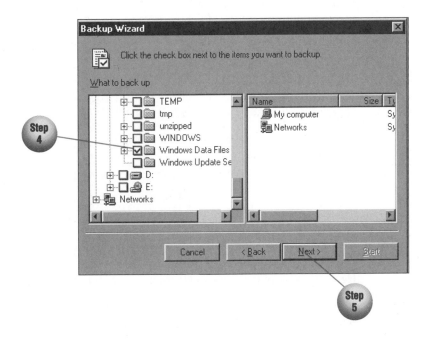

(continued)

Maintaining and Optimizing the Computer

6 You want to back up all the files in the *Windows Data Files* folder. Make sure the <u>A</u>ll selected files option is selected. Then click <u>N</u>ext.

The fourth window in the Backup Wizard is displayed. This window allows you to select a destination for the backup, that is, where the backup copies will be saved. The default option in the first box is File.

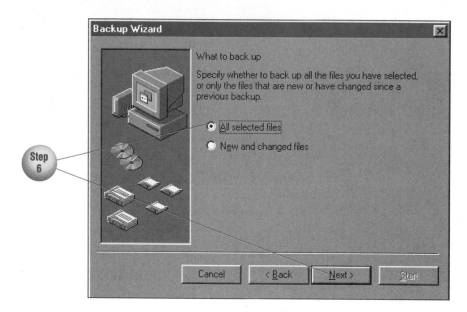

7 Accept the default location and place a floppy disk in drive A:.

For this exercise, the backup copy will be saved on a floppy disk in drive A:. This would be impractical if you were backing up the entire hard disk drive as it would take an enormous stack of floppy disks to save all the data.

8 Select whatever is entered in the second text box and key **a:** followed by today's date, with hyphens separating the month, day, and year. End the file name with the following extension: **.qic**.

There cannot be any spaces in the file name. All the files being copied are going to be saved as one file. The name of this backup file must end with the extension .qic.

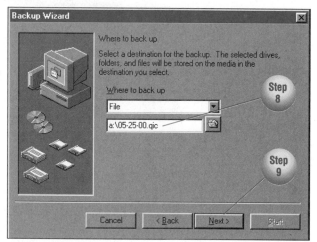

9 Write down this file name since you will need it in the following exercise. Then click <u>N</u>ext.

The fifth window in the Backup Wizard is displayed. This window enables you to select whether or not the original and backup copies will be compared to verify that the original data was backed up successfully and to select whether or not the backed up data will be compressed in order to save disk space.

10 Make sure both the verification and compression options are selected and then click Next.

The last window in the Backup Wizard is displayed. This window enables you to give the backup job a name. The name you give the backup job helps you keep track of different backups you make.

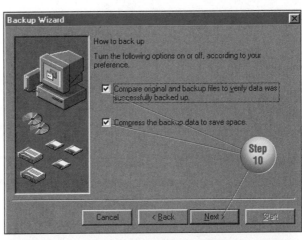

11 In the Type a name for this backup job text box, key the following: **Windows Data Files**.

12 Click the Start button.

In a moment, the Backup Progress window is displayed, reporting on such information as how much time has elapsed and the files currently being processed.

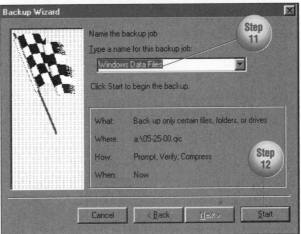

13 At the message that displays indicating that the operation is complete, click OK.

14 Click the Close button to close the Backup Progress window and the Microsoft Backup window.

Restoring a Backup

The Windows 98 Backup feature copies and compresses the files into a single file, which has a special format. If you want to retrieve some or all the files that were copied using the Backup command, you cannot simply copy them back to the hard disk. Instead, you must use the Restore feature that is part of the Backup command. With that feature, you can locate and select only certain files to restore, or you can restore the entire set.

steps

(Note: To complete this exercise, you will need the floppy disk with the backup files you made in the previous exercise.)

1. Place the floppy disk containing the backup files you made in the previous exercise in drive A:. Click the Start button on the Taskbar, point to Programs, point to Accessories, point to System Tools, and then click Backup.

2. At the Microsoft Backup window that displays, click the Restore backed up files option to select it and then click OK.

   The first window of the Restore Wizard is displayed. This window enables you to select the device to restore from. This would be the drive containing the disks or tapes on which the backup files are stored.

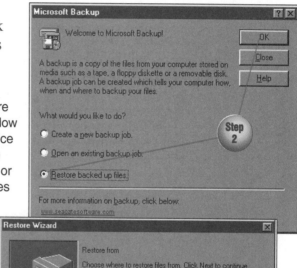

3. File should be entered in the first Restore from box. In the second Restore from box, enter the name you gave the file in step 7 of the previous exercise. Then click the Next button.

   The Select Backup Sets window is displayed. The *Windows Data Files* folder should already be selected.

4. Click OK.

   The first window of the Restore Wizard is displayed. You are asked to select the items you want to restore.

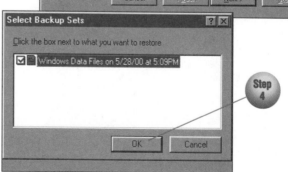

(5) Navigate to the *Windows Data Files* folder on drive C: and click the box next to it to select it. (There should be a blue checkmark in the box.)

(6) Click Next.

The second window of the Restore Wizard is displayed, asking you to specify where you want to restore the files.

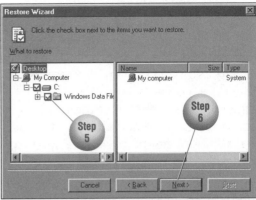

(7) You want to accept the default location for storing, which is Original Location. Click Next.

The third window of the Restore Wizard is displayed. You are asked how to restore the files. Table WIN5.1 explains each of these options.

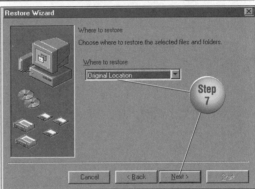

(8) The recommended restoring option is Do not replace the file on my computer. For this exercise, select the Always replace the file on my computer and then click Start.

(9) At the Media Required window that displays, click OK.

(10) At the message that displays indicating that the operation is complete, click OK.

(11) Click the Close button ☒ to close the Restore Progress window and the Microsoft Backup window.

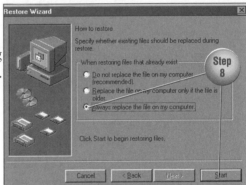

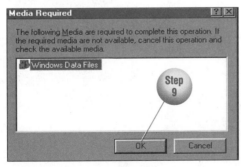

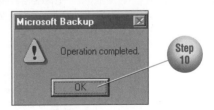

TABLE WIN5.1 Options for Restoring Files

Option	Explanation
Do not replace the file on my computer	Does not replace the files on the hard disk, even if the backed-up file is a more recent version than the file on the hard disk.
Replace the file on my computer only if the file is older	Replaces older files on the hard disk with more recent files of the same name from the backup set.
Always replace the file on my computer	Always replaces the files on the hard disk with files of the same name in the backup set, regardless of modification dates.

Making a Backup Copy
of a Floppy Disk

If you have a floppy disk that contains files, you can easily make a backup copy of the entire disk. Having two copies of any disk you use for your schoolwork is always a good idea. That way if you lose a disk you will always have a replacement. You will need two floppy disks to complete the following exercise. One of the disks should be blank. The second disk should have some data stored on it. The disk containing the files to be copied is called the *source disk*. The blank disk that will become the backup copy of the original disk is called the *destination disk*. When the computer accesses the files to be copied from the source disk, the process is called *reading from the disk*. When the computer copies those files onto the destination disk, the process is called *writing to* the disk.

steps

1. Place the floppy disk that has some data stored on it in drive A:. Double-click the *My Computer* icon.

2. Right-click the *3½ Floppy (A:)* icon.

3. From the shortcut menu that is displayed, click Copy Disk.

   The Copy Disk window is displayed, showing 3½ Floppy (A:) selected in both the Copy from and Copy to boxes.

4. Click Start.

   The Copy Disk window starts displaying the progress being made in reading the files from the source disk.

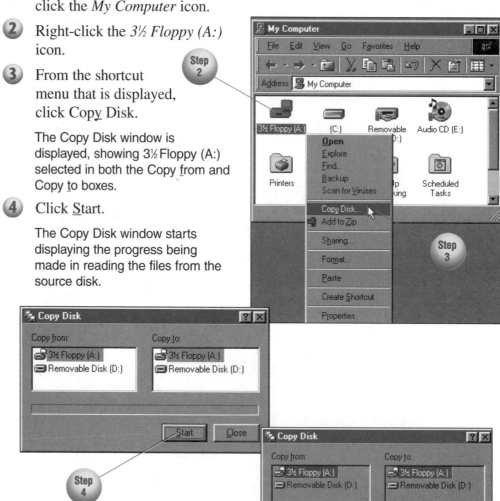

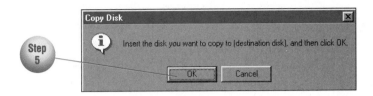

5 After a few moments, a window displays, prompting you to insert the disk you want to copy to. Remove the disk from drive A:, insert a blank disk into drive A:, and then click OK.

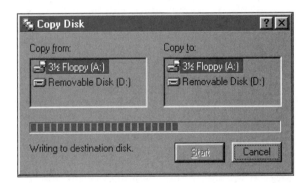

The Copy Disk window starts displaying the progress being made writing the files to the destination disk.

6 When the Copy Disk window reports that the disk has been successfully copied, click the Close button to quit.

7 Click the Close button ☒ to close the My Computer window.

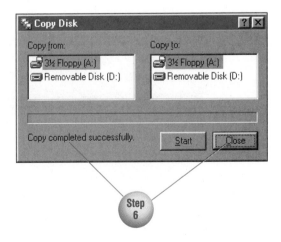

Using Data Compression

Data compression enables you to store data in a format that takes less space than usual. Windows 98 includes a data compression tool called DriveSpace 3 that can increase significantly the storage space for files. DriveSpace 3 can compress the data on both hard and floppy disks. You may want to consider using DriveSpace 3 to compress your files if your disk is starting to fill up. Backing up a disk before using any data compression utility is always a good idea, in case the data becomes corrupted during the compression process. In the following exercise you will compress the files on the backup disk you made in the previous exercise.

steps

(Warning: It could take up to an hour to complete the data compression procedure in this exercise. Once it is started, the data compression procedure cannot be canceled or stopped. Make sure you have plenty of time to complete this exercise.)

1. Place the backup copy of the disk that you made in the previous exercise in drive A:.

2. Double-click the *My Computer* icon.

3. Right-click the *3½ Floppy (A:)* icon.

4. Click Properties.

5. Write down the amount of used disk space and the amount of free disk space. Then click Cancel.

6. Click the Close button ☒ to close the My Computer window.

7. Click Start, point to Programs, point to Accessories, point to System Tools, and then click DriveSpace.

8. At the DriveSpace window that displays, click Drive A 3.5" Floppy drive to select it.

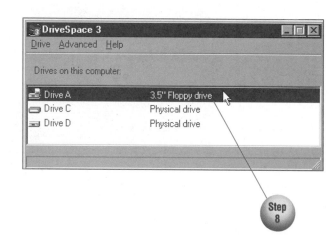

Step 8

⑨ Click <u>D</u>rive and then click <u>C</u>ompress.

The Compress a Drive window is displayed. The window shows you how much free space is currently on the disk and how much there will be once the disk is compressed.

⑩ At the Compress a Drive window, click <u>S</u>tart.

The window displays a warning that the procedure could take up to an hour. It also suggests you back up the files, which you have already done.

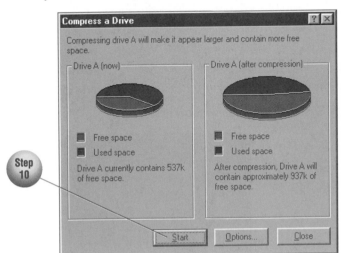

⑪ At the Are you sure? window that displays, click Compress <u>N</u>ow.

The Compress a Drive window reports on the progress of the procedure. When all the files on the disk have been compressed, the Compress a Drive window reports on how much space you gained by compressing the drive. Compare how much free space you now have on the disk with what you wrote down in step 5.

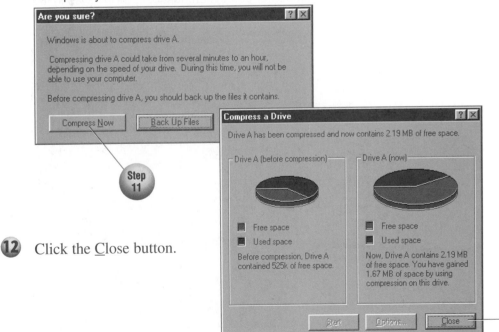

⑫ Click the <u>C</u>lose button.

Displaying System Properties

If something does go wrong with your computer and you have to contact a technician, he or she may need to gather some information about the components and size of your system. The System Properties window displays a detailed description about the computer system, including the operating system, the kind of computer you are using, the processor type, the amount of installed memory, and the devices attached to your computer. You will also find this information helpful if you are considering purchasing new software or special devices such as a scanner and a high-speed modem.

steps

① Right-click the *My Computer* icon and click P̲roperties.

The System Properties window is displayed.

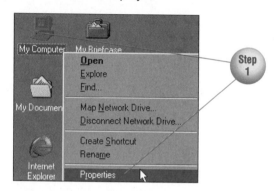

② If necessary, click the General tab.

The General tab on the System Properties window provides information such as the type of processor and the amount of RAM installed in the computer.

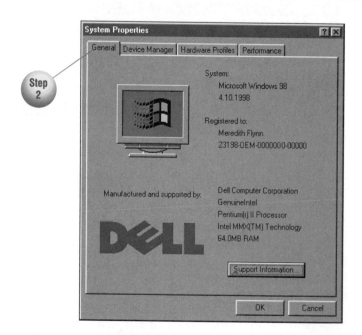

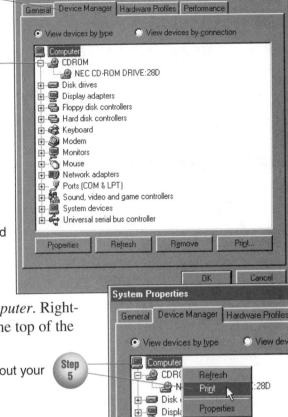

(3) Click the Device Manager tab.

The Device Manager tab on the System Properties window displays information on all the hardware devices installed on the computer.

(4) Click the plus sign next to CDROM to see the properties of your CD-ROM drive.

Clicking a plus sign displays information such as the type and size of that device.

(5) There may be times when you want a hard copy of the information about your *Computer*. Right-click the *Computer* icon at the top of the list and then click Print.

All the hardware information about your computer system is printed.

(6) Click the Performance tab.

The Performance tab on the System Properties window displays information on your computer's performance status such as the amount of memory, along with the size of certain performance components.

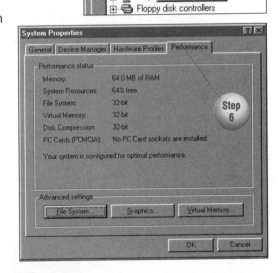

(7) Click the Close button ![X] to close the System Properties window.

Naming a Disk

On floppy disks, name labels can rub off. If you name a disk using the Windows 98 Properties feature, however, you will always be able to display the disk name. You might, for example, want to name a disk using your last name and the type of files that are saved on it. You can name a disk in either My Computer or Windows Explorer by right clicking the disk you want to name. Then click Properties on the shortcut menu. If necessary, click the General tab. In the Label box, enter a name for the disk. The name can have up to 11 characters. If you want to change an existing label, select it and enter a new name.

Take 2

Creating a Startup Disk

When you turn on your computer, it first checks the floppy drive for the files it needs to start up the computer. If it does not find those files in the floppy drive, it then checks the hard drive for them. That way, if something were wrong with your hard drive you still would be able to start the computer using a floppy disk. Simply place the startup disk in the floppy drive and the computer would start from that disk, not from the hard drive. You can create a startup floppy disk using options in the Control Panel window, which is accessed through the Start button and then Settings.

steps

(Note: For the following exercise you will need a disk with at least 1.2 MB capacity for creating the startup disk.)

1. Click the Start button on the Taskbar, point to <u>S</u>ettings, and click <u>C</u>ontrol Panel.

2. At the Control Panel window that displays, double-click *Add/Remove Programs*.

   The Add/Remove Programs Properties window is displayed.

3. Click the Startup Disk tab.

4. Click the <u>C</u>reate Disk button.

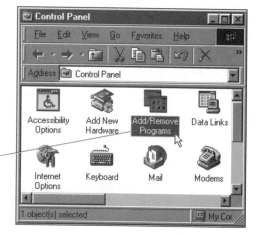

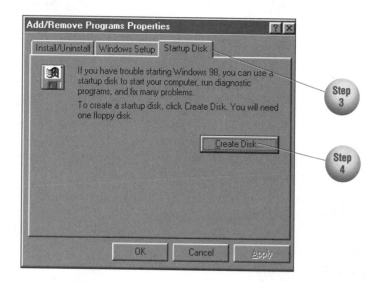

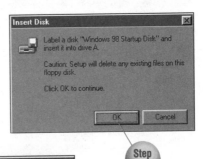

5 At the window that displays instructing you to insert a floppy disk in drive A:, place a blank floppy disk in drive A: and then click the OK button.

The Add/Remove Programs Properties window displays the progress the computer is making in creating the startup disk.

Step 5

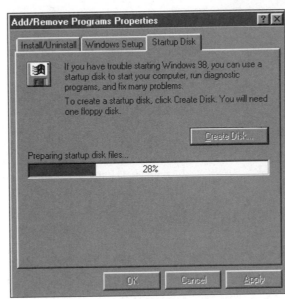

6 Once the disk has been created, remove the Windows 98 startup disk from drive A: and click the Close button ✕ to close the Add/Remove Programs Properties window.

7 Click the close button ✕ to close the Control Panel window.

Removing Programs

Another way to free up space on your hard drive is to remove programs that you no longer use. Programs that were designed for Windows can be removed using the Add/Remove Programs Properties dialog box. Click Start on the Taskbar, point to Settings, click Control Panel, and then double-click Add/Remove Programs. Click the name of the program you want to remove and then click the Add/Remove button. Make absolutely certain you want to remove the selected program before clicking the Add/Remove button.

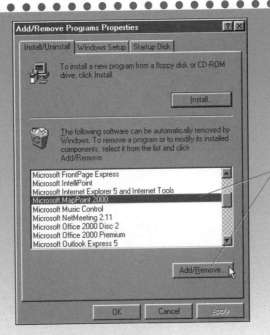

Click the program you want to remove and then click the Add/Remove button

Take 2

Maintaining and Optimizing the Computer

Features Summary

Action	Steps
Back up data files	Click the Start button, point to Programs, point to Accessories, point to System Tools, click Backup
Compress the data on a disk	Click the Start button, point to Programs, point to Accessories, point to System Tools, click DriveSpace
Create a startup disk	Click the Start button, point to Settings, click Control Panel, double-click the *Add/Remove Programs* icon, click the Startup Disk tab, click Create Disk
Defragment the hard drive	Click the Start button, point to Programs, point to Accessories, point to System Tools, click Disk Defragmenter
Delete unnecessary files	Click the Start button, point to Programs, point to Accessories, point to System Tools, click Disk Cleanup
Display disk properties	Double-click *My Computer* icon, right-click icon for disk, click Properties
Display system properties	Right-click the *My Computer* icon, click Properties
Make a backup copy of a floppy disk	Double-click the *My Computer* icon, right-click the icon for the 3½ Floppy (A:) drive, click Copy Disk
Restore backup files	Click the Start button, point to Programs, point to Accessories, point to System Tools, click Backup
Scan a disk for errors	Click the Start button, point to Programs, point to Accessories, point to System Tools, click ScanDisk
Use the Maintenance Wizard	Click the Start button, point to Programs, point to Accessories, point to System Tools, click Maintenance Wizard

Procedures Check

Completion: In the space provided at the right, indicate the correct term, icon, button, or command.

1. After right-clicking the icon for a disk drive from the My Computer window, click this option from the shortcut menu to display the amount of available disk space. _____

2. This is an example of the type of file that can be deleted using Disk Cleanup. _____

3. The ScanDisk command can check your hard disk drive for these two things.

   _____

   _____

4. The name of the storage locations on a disk in which a file is saved. _____

5. This term describes a file that is saved in noncontiguous locations on the hard drive. _____

6. The Maintenance Wizard combines these three Windows 98 commands.

   _____

   _____

   _____

7. The name of a backup file created with the Windows 98 Backup command must end with this extension. _____

8. To retrieve a file that was copied using the Backup command, use this feature. _____

9. This term describes the disk containing the files to be copied during a backup of a floppy disk. _____

10. This term describes the disk onto which the original files are copied during a backup copy of a floppy disk. _____

11. If you want to know the amount of RAM installed in a computer, right-click this icon and then click Properties. _____

12. When the computer is turned on, this is the first place it looks for the files it needs to start up. _____

Skills Review

Activity 1: Displaying Disk Properties

1. Double-click the *My Computer* icon.
2. Right click the icon for the hard disk drive.
3. From the shortcut menu, click Properties.
4. What is the storage capacity of the disk?
5. Close the Properties window. Close the My Computer window.
6. Display the amount of free space on the startup disk you created in the last exercise (before the "Features Summary"). Place the Startup disk in drive A:. Double-click the *My Computer* icon.
7. Right-click the icon for the floppy disk drive.
8. From the shortcut menu, click Properties.
9. How much free space is on the startup disk?
10. Close the Properties window. Close the My Computer window.

Activity 2: Cleaning Up the Hard Disk

1. Click the Start button, point to Programs, point to Accessories, point to System Tools, and then click Disk Cleanup.
2. Select drive C: as the drive you want to clean up.
3. Select Temporary Internet Files, Downloaded Program Files, Offline Web Pages, Recycle Bin, and Temporary Files as the files to be deleted. Click OK.
4. Click Yes when the window is displayed asking if you are sure you want to delete files.

Activity 3: Checking a Floppy Disk for Errors

1. Place a floppy disk in drive A:.
2. Click the Start button, point to Programs, point to Accessories, point to System Tools, and click ScanDisk.
3. Select 3½ Floppy (A:) as the drive you want to check.
4. Select the Thorough option.
5. Click Start.
6. When the process is completed, close the ScanDisk Results window. Close the ScanDisk window.

Activity 4: Compressing Data

(Note: Before completing these steps, make sure the Windows Data Files *folder and its contents are available on your computer's hard drive. This folder can be downloaded from the EMC/Paradigm Web site, or you may get it from your instructor.)*

1 Copy the *Windows Data Files* folder on your computer's hard drive to a floppy disk.
2 Click Start, point to Programs, point to Accessories, point to System Tools, and then click DriveSpace.
3 Select drive A: as the drive you want to compress.
4 Click Drive and then click Compress.
5 Click Start.
6 When the Are you sure? window is displayed, click Compress Now.
7 When the Compress a Drive window is displayed, look to see how much space you gained by compressing the drive. Click the Close button.
8 Click the Close button to the DriveSpace 3 window.

Performance Plus

Activity 1: Finding Information on How to Uncompress Files

1 Use the Help menu in the DriveSpace 3 window to find out how you uncompress a drive. Use WordPad to list the step-by-step directions for uncompressing a file. Print the directions. You do not need to save the file.
2 Use your directions to uncompress the files you compressed in Activity 4: Compressing Data. When the Remove Compression? window is displayed, click No.
3 When the uncompress process is completed, close the Uncompress a Drive window and close the DriveSpace 3 window.

Activity 2: Making a Backup Copy of a Floppy Disk

1 You will need the disk with the uncompressed Windows Data Files you created in the previous activity and a blank floppy disk. Place the disk with the uncompressed Windows Data Files in drive A:.
2 Copy the disk in drive A: to the blank floppy disk.
3 When the disk is copied, close any open windows.

Activity 3: Defragmenting a Disk

1 Place the backup copy of the Windows Data Files that you created in Performance Plus Activity 2 in drive A:.
2 Use the Windows 98 Disk Defragmenter to defragment the floppy disk in drive A.: When the defragmentation process starts, click the Show Details button.
3 When the disk has been defragmented, quit Disk Defragmenter.

Activity 4: Creating a Startup Disk

1 Put a blank floppy disk in drive A:.
2 From the Start menu, point to Settings and click Control Panel. Double-click Add/Remove Programs.
3 Click the Startup Disk tab and create a startup disk.
4 Once the startup disk has been created, close any open windows.
5 To complete Activity 5, you will need to copy the files on the startup disk to a folder you create on the Desktop. Use Windows Explorer to create a new folder on drive C:. Name the folder Startup. If you need help creating a folder, refer to Section 2 "Managing Files and Customizing Windows."
6 Use Windows Explorer to copy the files on the floppy disk in drive A: to the *Startup* folder you just created on drive C:. If you need help on copying files, refer to Section 2, "Managing Files and Customizing Windows."

Activity 5: Backing Up and Restoring Files

1 Place a blank floppy disk in drive A:.
2 Use the Windows 98 Backup command to back up the files in the Startup folder on drive C. You created this folder and copied files into it in Activity 4. Back up all the files in the Startup folder. Back the files up to the blank floppy disk in drive A:. Give the file an appropriate name, such as today's date. Name the backup job Startup Files.
3 When the operation is complete, close all open windows. View the contents of the floppy disk in drive A: to make sure the backup file is there.
4 Use the Windows 98 Backup command to restore the files on the floppy disk in drive A: to their original location, which is the *Startup* folder on drive C:. The option Always replace the file on my computer should be selected.
5 When the operation is complete, close all open windows.
6 Use Windows Explorer to drag the *Startup* folder from the C: drive to the Recycle Bin.